UNSEENPRESS.COM'S OFFICIAL

ENCYCLOPEDIA OF

HAUNTED

CENTRAL

INDIANA

BY
NICOLE KOBROWSKI

Unseenpress.com, Inc. PO Box 687 Westfield, IN 46074

UNSEENPRESS.COM'S OFFICIAL

ENCYCLOPEDIA OF

HAUNTED

CENTRAL

INDIANA

BY
NICOLE KOBROWSKI

Unseenpress.com, Inc. PO Box 687 Westfield, IN 46074

For information contact:
Unseenpress.com, Inc.
PO Box 687
Westfield, IN 46074

Library of Congress Cataloging-in-Publication Data

Kobrowski, Nicole
   Unseenpress.com's Definitive Encyclopedia of Haunted Central Indiana/Nicole Kobrowski
          Includes index
  1. Ghosts Indiana; 2. Paranormal Indiana; 3. Indiana History; 4. Indiana Travel

Library of Congress Control Number: 2017900823
ISBN-13: 978-0-9986207-2-5

Printed in the United States of America

Published by
Haunted Backroads Books
an imprint of Unseenpress.com, Inc.
PO Box 687
Westfield, IN 46074

Although the authors and publisher have made every effort to ensure the accuracy and completeness of information contained in this book, we assume no responsibility for errors, inaccuracies, omissions or any inconsistency herein. Any slights of people, places or organizations are unintentional.

The Unseenpress.com, Inc. website is
http://www.unseenpress.com/

Cover design Unseenpress.com, Inc.

NOTES

The persons, events, places and incidents depicted in this book are based on oral history, memoirs, interviews and accounts that were used as research for this book. The author makes no claim as to the veracity of the information. The author makes no claim as to the exact historical authenticity of the legends presented in this book. The author does not guarantee any location directions contained in this book. You visit these sites at your own risk. Although many sites are open to visitors during the day (and some in the evening), they all have an owner.

Additionally, this book is comprised of material that is intended for the entertainment of its readers. The author has paid particular attention to collecting legends that have been told, in many cases, for generations. The information concerning these legends may not reflect historical events. The author takes no responsibility for the veracity of each story except that she believes the storytellers. The author has attempted to research and locate each area as accurately as possible. Although we made every effort to ensure that the information was correct at the time the book went to press, we do not assume and hereby disclaim any liability to any party for loss, damage, or injury caused by information contained in this book. Furthermore the publishers disclaim any liability resulting from the use of this book. The publishers and author do not condone, advise, or recommend visiting these sites without obtaining permission first and taking safety precautions.

We apologize if there is inaccurate information presented in the book and will rectify future additions and editions if we are contacted by mail or email and provided the correct information.

Table of Contents

OTHER TITLES BY NICOLE KOBROWSKI

Published by Unseenpress.com, Inc.
(print and ebook)

- Haunted Backroads: Central Indiana
- Haunted Backroads: Ghosts of Westfield
- Haunted Backroads: Ghosts of Madison County, Indiana
- Fractured Intentions: A History of Central State Hospital for the Insane
- She Sleeps Well: The Extraordinary Life and Murder of Dr. Helene Elise Hermine Knabe
- Unseenpress.com's Official Encyclopedia of Haunted Indiana
- Unseenpress.com's Official Encyclopedia of Haunted Northern Indiana
- Unseenpress.com's Official Encyclopedia of Haunted Central Indiana
- Unseenpress.com's Official Encyclopedia of Haunted Southern Indiana

Published by IUPUI
Distance Learning: A Guide to System Planning and Implementation
(by Merrill, Young, and Kobrowski)

Published by Bildungsverlag EINS
Metal Line (Instructor's guide and workbook)
Hotel Line (Instructor's Guide)
Englisch für Elektroberufe (Instructor's guide and workbook)
Supply Line (Instructor's guide and workbook)
Construction Line (Instructor's guide and workbook)

Coming soon!
Haunted Backroads: Ghosts of Hamilton County, Indiana
Audio books

DEDICATION

*To Michael, because it was late
and he was crabby
and he thought he should have a dedication.*

ABOUT THE AUTHOR

Nicole Kobrowski is the co-owner of Unseenpress.com, Inc., which was founded in 2001. She and her husband Michael started the business because of their interest in the paranormal and their love of history. She has written professionally under a variety of pen names for over 20 years, including books for ESL and dozens of articles on a myriad topics. Being a paranormal enthusiast for over 30 years, she has done investigation work in many areas including spirit photography, electronic voice phenomenon, and automatic writing. In addition to her work in the paranormal field, Nicole is an Adult Education Consultant. Currently, she lives in her "über haunted home" with her husband and Lyla, their rescued cat.

Preface

Every book I write is a creative pleasure. With this particular book, I need to learn to cut the cord. Every time I was about to finish and send it off, someone (sometimes me) would let me know about another fascinating place that I think just has to be included.

When I originally wrote the book, I had been to about 33% of these locations. As of this writing, I have been to over 70%. By the next writing, I will have completed my goal of visiting every site listed.

As always, the intent of this book is to educate and to serve as a guide for paranormal enthusiasts, investigators and anyone traveling around the wonderful state of Indiana.

Special thanks to Emily Dickos-Carter and to Megan Norris.

I hope you enjoy it as much as I enjoyed writing it.

Nicole Kobrowski
January 2017

We love hearing from paranormal enthusiasts and investigators about their experiences at these locations or from other "haunted' locations. Send all enquiries or story submissions for future publications to customerservice@ unseenpress.com.

A Guide to the Encyclopedia

This book is set up in order for you to find information quickly and easily. The book is set up by counties, which you'll find at the top of each page. For each entry, I've developed a legend for your use as follows:

Sample Entry

Abner Longley Park	The name of the location.
Lebanon: 1601 Longley Drive	The directions, address and supporting information.
Abner Longley Park was named for the founder of Lebanon. Follow the trail into the woods. People into the occult have set up an altar of sorts. A negative presence permeates the woods. Dark, sinister shadow figures appear and follow visitors. One visitor was scratched across the face.	The section entry contains background on events around the history and haunting.

Do-It-Yourself Investigations

Since starting Unseenpress.com, Inc. we've been approached by people and organizations on a weekly basis asking us if we'd investigate their home or asking if they can go with us to a "ghost hunt" or an "investigation". These aren't even including the places we approach for investigations. Unfortunately, we can't accommodate all requests- days only have 24 hours. As a result, we've referred some people to reputable paranormal groups so they connect with investigators in their area and we've worked with clients to find them reputable help in their area. Also, we have taken some experienced investigators on our investigations and had great success with it. We have also started education classes for people who want to take responsibility for their own hauntings. We'll talk more about that later.

Still, we find a fundamental difference in some of the requests- "ghost hunt" and "investigation". Both terms have very different meanings. Certain people want to go to haunted locations, be scared, talk about what they've experienced, make a quick determination it is haunted (or not) and move on to the next location. Other people want to conduct investigations that are scientifically documented, following set procedures.

Before you go

Your team should have a clear idea of who they are and how they should behave before they ever set foot on the client's property. Standards should be explained and reviewed before the investigation.

Before you decide to go, we recommend the following standards:

- Get permission (See Permission section).
- Walk the area before the investigation. If you're doing a daytime investigation, this is not so important. If you're doing a night time investigation, you should do this step to understand where you might encounter difficulty. You should always do a walk through to understand the temperature fluctuations and EMF readings (however, how will you really know what a baseline is? You could be experiencing paranormal activity on your first visit).
- Meet at the location and decide who will do what and with what equipment.
- Offer a blessing, protection, or prayer if you wish.
- Walk around to decide where to place equipment.
- Take pictures, videos and audio recordings. Make notes about any changes in temperature, feelings you had or sightings. If everyone on your team does this, you should have an accurate picture of the investigation when you're finished. It helps eliminate non-paranormal causes for suspected activity.

Once you've made the necessary arrangements, consider the following points during an investigation.

- Never roam alone in an unfamiliar setting. You need to be safe.
- Take ID with you. You might need to prove who you are.
- Take a cell phone with you and let others know where you are going.
- If you will be in the field for a long time, take adequate food and drink with you. Eat only in specific areas to minimize noise and contamination of evidence.
- If you are asked to leave, do so without making a fuss. It will benefit you in the long run. Respect everyone

living and dead.
- Don't smoke. It can contaminate photographic/video evidence.
- Use care when taking photos. Don't take photos when others are taking them. Note anything that could create false orbs in photos. Keep hair, fingers and camera straps away from the lens. You, equipment, or other items can cast false positive shadows so be aware of your location and equipment placement.
- Do not move audio recorders when speaking. It can create distortion.
- No drugs or alcohol before, during or after an investigation. If you're sick, stay home. Illegal drugs are a no. Drunk people on an investigation or after an investigation while still a part of the team is stupid and not good for the paranormal field or its image.
- Record any conditions that could affect data (humidity, dust, etc.).
- No noisy clothing, jewelry, keys, or change- these items affect what we hear.
- Apply no items that affect smell- cologne, perfume, etc. Do use fragrance-free deodorant.
- Dress for the field. Use your team's uniform or wear clean, weather appropriate clothes.
- Ensure hair is away from face- ponytails are good. Buns are even better.
- If you are frightened in a location- leave. Some of the most haunted places are in the middle of nowhere and you might have a bad encounter with a human. Use common sense.
- Have an emergency plan and make sure someone is on the team that is able to perform CPR and/or call for help quickly.

Paranormal Investigation

The Field
Much information is written about paranormal investigation. Some of it is stated in absolute terms. Paranormal investigation is a wide open field. I say field, because that is what it should be, however, to my knowledge, no one makes a living solely by investigating the paranormal- myself included. Certainly, research labs exist for parapsychology, which is completely different than paranormal investigation. Most investigators belong to organizations that support paranormal research, though, most everyone has a day job.

Education Options
Along these same lines, there are no accredited degrees in paranormal investigation. None. Zero. Nada. Niet, Kein. Don't even waste your time and money. Many paranormal organizations offer certificate courses to become "certified" in paranormal investigation. Many paranormal groups charge dues and ask you to take classes (sometimes paying extra) in order to be "qualified" to go on investigations. As a lifelong student of Adult Education, I can hardly argue about basic training needed to safely go on an investigation. However, each organization has its own policies and procedures for accomplishing an investigation. You have to decide if they are sound, if you agree with them and if you'd like to be a part of the organization.

Knowing the state of education in the paranormal field, this difference begs the question, "what does being a certified paranormal investigator (or obtaining a certificate) get me? Some people believe it doesn't really benefit you. As it isn't a recognized field of work or science (yes, we are considered pseudo-scientists), it isn't going to raise your pay (unless you latch onto the media). Some people would argue the benefit comes in being certified to investigate with the organization that certified you. Other people argue that being certified or recognized by a certain group is motivation enough. They believe that this certification might get them into more places or give them more of an advantage. Again, it is up to your interpretation.

Media, Myths and Absolutes

No one, no matter what experiences someone has had with the paranormal, knows what to expect or what concrete facts can be said about spirit activity. No one can concretely define what a ghost really is or if they exist. While I have definitions of some of the elements surrounding the paranormal and investigation, my take may be different than another investigator's definition. Also, I have most definite feelings about ghosts; I am a firm believer in them. Some people are out to disprove the existence of spirits.

The media also has its own take on the paranormal ranging from the cheesy "ghostbusters" type attitude to making it somewhat darker and more dramatic than what it really is. For example, shows exist for ratings. If television shows didn't have something scary and exciting, no one would watch them. Be careful what you consume.

Also, be careful about what you read and absorb. For example, an investigator on a popular television series said "A human spirit can only lift three to ten pounds." Really? How do we know this? Did this investigator have an interview with a ghost? Because if he did, I would love the transcript. Does this mean that when Arnold Schwarzenegger dies he is limited to lifting three to ten pounds? Or does he get to lift more because he was a body builder? Likewise another misconception is that the "haunting hours" are between 12-3am. If that were true, why do we have so many daytime reports of activity?

Absolute statements like the ones above are patently false until proven otherwise. If someone says conclusively, "Yep, you've got ghosts.", it is their own flavor and opinion- kind of like a certification that your house is haunted. Other investigators may disagree with the findings. While some people believe that ghosts can go home with you (as I do), there are other investigators who do not believe this.

If we can't prove anything what is the point?

All we can do is conduct inquiry based on common assumptions and draw our own conclusions. However, surrounding investigative inquiry is more than just our opinions and biases. We also must take scientific method into account. In scientific inquiry, we decide what we're going to study, decide on an explanation for what we're studying, define how we'll research it, muse on the types of results you think you'll get, execute and analyze the plan. Scientific method is scientific method, no matter what area you are in. I am a scholar in Adult Education and I apply scientific method the same as anyone who has learned it. The focus of my research in Adult Education is different than that of a Sociologist.

You might ask what the problem is, that scientific inquiry seems very straightforward. It is, but what is contained in each step is the difference between mainstream, accepted science and the assumed pseudo-science of the paranormal. We can't test against what we don't know. Our tools have only been test driven to a certain point. For example, many investigators believe EMF detectors can indicate spirit activity. How do we know they aren't picking up power inside the walls, under the floor, etc.? There is a scale for what is normal for certain types of electromagnetic fields, but have we been able to consistently replicate what we're seeing as "abnormal" to be able to say it is truly abnormal and paranormal?

Organizations and Investigations

Investigators employ several steps involved in paranormal investigation. Investigations aren't always exciting and many of them are hurry up and wait situations. Sometimes you get a hit and sometimes after hours of sitting or hours of analyzing, you get nothing. It can be frustrating, but also rewarding. The difference amoung investigators is how they conduct themselves, their groups and their investigations.

One bad experience can lead to a complete distaste for the paranormal in general. Two recent cases come to mind. First, the producers of a show about ghost children did an unauthorized ghost hunt and filiming in Crown Hill Cemetery in Indianapolis, Indiana. While I believe there is much paranormal activity afoot in the cemetery, the cemetery staff made it quite clear that it wants nothing to do with the paranormal. The makers of the program misrepresented the history of the subject and also the history of Crown Hill. Additionally, they didn't ask permission to film on the grounds. They seemed to assume that because it was a cemetery, owned by the State (not true), it was fair game (also not true).

Another example is Central State Hospital also in Indianapolis. A "documentary" was produced on the premise that it would be historic in nature. It was historic all right, but not the historic documentary that was presented in the proposal to the city. Would you want to be affiliated with an organization that misrepresents itself?

Reputation

Moving to the practical, keep in mind that the reputation of your organizations, investigations, and personal behavior is under scrutiny from the minute you approach an organization or individual about conducting an investigation. How you conduct your organization, investigations and/or personal behavior determine how much credibility each element has and how the paranormal community is perceived as a whole. For example, a group of investigators trespassed on a site where a well known serial killer lived. They took pictures and video and posted both on their website and a video sharing site. They even boasted about it on television. When the owner saw this evidence, the police became involved. What do you think about this group's ethics or credibility? I certainly wouldn't want to work with this group. Another group trespassed at Central State Hospital, several times. They were told by the police to stay away from the site but didn't. Now, they have a bad reputation with the police and have given paranormal investigation a bad name. Would you want these people coming into your home or business?

Permission

Investigation doesn't mean glory. Too many times have I seen investigators jockey for position while investigating hauntings. With the exception of private homes, businesses, etc. any already known location has been investigated or hunted to some extent many time over. There is no "scooping" going on. For example, Central State Hospital in Indianapolis is the perceived as the Holy Grail of haunted locations. Who hasn't been out there? Most folks who have been here are employees, with the police or have done so illegally. What does claiming "first rights" do? Absolutely nothing. What does the trespassing do to the credibility of you, your organization and to the field? *Trespassing kills credibility.*

Many people say, "well how do you get in there?" or "I don't know how to get permission." Well, here's your guide. Find the owner and get permission. *Always get it in writing.*

Find the Owner
Property, including businesses, historic properties, "abandoned" properties, farms, woods, etc.

Go to the township or county recorder and ask for the name of the owner on record for the property. This is public information that they have to give you. You can usually get a phone number as well. Contact the owners and if they don't respond, follow up. If they still don't respond or you get a resounding, "No," let it go. Remember, what you do and how you act reflects on not just you and your organization, but on everyone. Think about how you can revisit it at a future time and maybe change the no to a yes.

Cemeteries
Go to the township trustee, who usually controls them. If your county has a cemetery commission, speak with them. If it is a large cemetery like Crown Hill that is run by an organization, talk to them. If it is a cemetery attached to a church, talk to the pastor, minister, priest, etc. Don't assume that because it is a cemetery that you can visit it any time you wish. Most cemeteries in Indiana close at dusk. Simply calling the police to let them know you're out there doesn't cover you. It is still under the control of others.

Roads and Highways
For your own safety, if nothing else, you must have permission to create an obstruction or to be on these roads. If you are walking on the road, you run the risk of getting yourself killed. If you're with several people, you increase your risk. Many of the haunted roads are in areas where people live.

Once an organized ghost hunting group decided to trespass on a fairly well known area in Hamilton County. They even posted pictures on the internet showing them trespassing. The police were alerted by the owner and they received a notice telling them to take down all photos, videos, etc and that next time they would be prosecuted. How would you like to ask the boss at your day job for bail money?

County Map

The map on the following page shows a numbered county map. On the next page, these numbers correspond with the correct county.

Use the names as a quick reference to find the correct county in the book.

COUNTY MAP OF INDIANA

ALPHABETICAL LIST OF INDIANA COUNTIES

Number	Name	Number	Name
6	Boone	49	Marion
12	Clinton	54	Montgomery
18	Delaware	55	Morgan
21	Fayette	61	Parke
23	Fountain	67	Putnam
29	Hamilton	68	Randolph
30	Hancock	70	Rush
32	Hendricks	73	Shelby
33	Henry	80	Tipton
34	Howard	81	Union
41	Johnson	83	Vermillion
48	Madison	89	Wayne

BOONE COUNTY

302 East Church Street
Thorntown: 302 E. Church St.

This second Empire home haunted by resident spirits who push visitors down stairs. Locals see lights from uncovered windows although there is no electricity connected to the home.

1424 Park Drive
Lebanon: 1424 Park Dr.

The ghost of a woman named Alexa haunts this home. It is believed she was murdered and buried in the sump pump well. She walks through the house and the basement as though she still lived there. This residual haunting seems to take place in the 1970s judging from her clothes. She is described as Latino and enjoys pets, especially cats.

Two other spirits inhabit the house. Jacob, a young boy sits in the bathroom and cries. Frank, a poltergeist who does not like the other two spirits, haunts the basement and throws things.

Additionally, a dark presence of an older man haunts the back yard. He looks in the windows from time to time and dislikes a messy yard.

7629 Stonegate Lane
Zionsville: 7629 Stonegate Lane

The Carolina Restaurant purchased an antique bar that is haunted by the spirit of a female bartender. She changes channels and music. She also enjoys making the lights flicker.

Abner Longley Park
Lebanon: 1601 Longley Drive

Abner Longley Park was named for the founder of Lebanon. Follow the trail into the woods. People into the occult have set up an altar of sorts. A negative presence permeates the woods. Dark, sinister shadow figures appear and follow visitors. One visitor was scratched across the face.

Boone County Courthouse
Lebanon: Bounded by SR 32, W. Main St., N. Meridian St., and W. Washington St.

Public hangings were held here. People hear the ghosts of several hanged victims screaming. Investigators see the corpses and ropes in mid-air, hear screaming and feel cold ghosts of wind in the basement.

Brown's Wonder Cemetery
Elizaville: Elizaville Rd. and 300 N

Since 1924, a seven foot tall man is seen between Elizaville and Lebanon. He is seen also in Brown's Wonder Cemetery. Legend says he is looking for something but can't find it. He has no issues with trying to take you back to where ever he stays. One evening, a visitor reported seeing the man and before he could move, talk, or leave, the mysterious figure came toward him. That is all the visitor remembered until he woke up, laid out on a grave in the cemetery. Digital movie and photo cameras with fresh batteries go dead.

Country Side Antiques
Thorntown: 4889 N. US 52

A customer swears that she went into this location and saw a series of pictures of a family ranging from the parents in high school to their wedding and the arrival of their children. She said she wanted to buy just a couple pictures but was overwhelmed with sadness when she picked just the ones she wanted that she put them down and refused to buy them. As she walked through the store, she was followed by one of the children in the picture and the boy held her hand.

Holiday Drive Bridge
(aka Screaming Bridge)
Zionsville: Located on the left side off of North Michigan Rd. past Willow Rd. Turn left on Neal Rd. (It is called Neal Rd., O'Neal Rd., and Holiday Rd.)

A lynching by the KKK took place on this isolated bridge. Screams, believed to be from the hanged man sound out in the late night.

Intersection of US 421 and SR 32
Lebanon: Intersection of SR 421 and SR 32

Several nuns died in a car accident. Investigators have seen their dark figures in a straight line moving from one side of the road to the others. One investigator was driving to the intersection when a truck in front of him slammed its brakes on. She didn't think she would be able to stop in time. She saw the nuns walk in between her car and the back of the truck. Her car immediately came to a dead stop.

Oak Hill Cemetery
Lebanon: Off E. Main St. south of E. Washington St.
(See Sylvia Likens, Indianapolis, Marion Co.)

The ghost of Sylvia Likens can be seen here. Sylvia was brutally killed in Indianapolis while in the care of the Baniszewski family. She was beaten and tortured for many months before her death. Sylvia walks through the cemetery and sometime leaves it, walking toward Indianapolis. Some people speculate she's walking back for revenge, although many of her torturers are long since dead. Other people theorize she's walking home to her biological family.

Old Indiana Fun Park
Thorntown: Intersection of SR 47 and I-65. Go west on to CR N350W and Kent Rd. (CR 700N)

Emily Hunt was paralyzed from the chest down and her grandmother, Nancy Jones, was killed after a train derailed at Old Indiana Fun Park. After a lengthy legal battle, the park closed. Today, it is a wildlife preserve.

Investigators report a residual haunting of the event with screams heard. In December 2007 a hunter saw "an older woman in white" walking through the park. He watched her come closer to him and as the hazy figure approached, she smiled and disappeared.

Old Lebanon High School
Lebanon:327 N Lebanon St.

Visitors claim to be trapped inside the building for several minutes to several hours at a time. Some people believe the building is conducive to time travel as they have seen people in clothes and heard music from other time periods.

Old Thorntown Graveyard
Thorntown: Bevel Rd. between N. Front St. and E. Pearl St.

People have been punched, scratched and touched in this cemetery. EVPs recorded document some unfriendly spirits asking people to leave "or else".

Witham Hospital
Lebanon: Hospital is at 2605 N. Lebanon St. The old Nurse's School is at 1122 N. Lebanon St. on the west side of the road.

Conceived in 1915, Witham hospital has been providing healthcare to the community for over 100 years. Staff and visitors report the ghosts of patient and former employees roaming the halls and in the old nurse's building, phantom nurses are seen often. Additionally, lights are said to turn off and on regularly with no explanation.

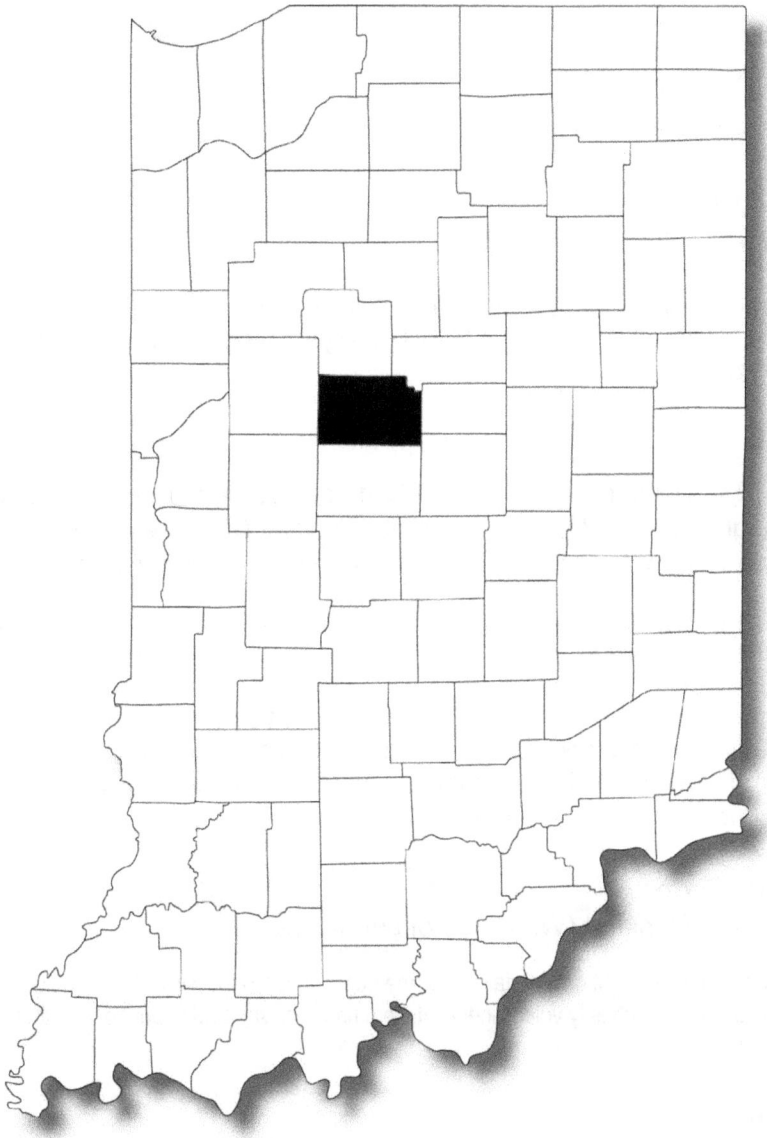

CLINTON
COUNTY

Clinton County Historical Society and Museum
Frankfort: 301 E. Clinton St.
(aka Old Stoney)

People hear voices and footsteps as well as see shadows and mysterious orbs.

Farmers Gravel Road
Frankfort: Farmers Gravel Rd.

In the early 1920s a school bus full of children was involved in an accident. Everyone on board died. If you stop and put your car in neutral, children push you up the hill (presumably to have you go down the hill and into the river). After, handprints are visible on your car.

Hamilton Road
Mulberry: Take SR 38 to Mulberry and CR 900W. If you are coming from Lafayette, go right on it and go through the next stop sign, which is Hamilton Rd. Three one-lane bridges are on this road. When you get to the third bridge, stop and flash your lights 4 times.

A church caught fire on this road in the 1800s and everyone inside was killed. Also, a set of railroad tracks are haunted by a boy named Danny, who was killed in the early 1910s. A cemetery near the railroad tracks is also haunted.

At the eastern-most bridge, you may be chased by an apparition of a man. Sometimes he's seen as a shadow and other times as a solid form. Park at the back of the cemetery, and you'll see flames from the woods and smell smoke. Visit the tracks, and you'll hear a train whistle and a very loud noise as if the train hit something. Sometimes Danny can be seen walking along the tracks as a transparent glowing apparition.

Main Street Pub and Eatery
Frankfort: 58 N. Main St. Frankfort (West side of courthouse)

A ghostly man sits at the bar. A chandelier light on the stairway to the upper floor swings wildly though no one can reach it. Lights turn off and on. Employees hear ghostly voices in the kitchen, back hallway, and upper floor as though unseen people are having a conversation.

Providence Cemetery
Mulberry: CR N580W outside of Mulberry

The church burned down years ago. Now, the church mysteriously reappears and screams are heard about 2 a.m. Visitors observe mists and experience physical contact (touches on neck, arms and shoulders).

Sleepy Hollow

Frankfort: Take CR 600W off Mulberry Jefferson Rd. (Wildcat Creek Bridge)
(aka Haunted Railroad Bridge/Trestle)

Kids were killed at this location. Their handprints appear on your car. The wooden railroad bridge is guarded by the ghosts of two dogs and a man. The man, who appears as a shadow figure, chases you out with the dogs.

A woman from the 1940s who killed herself because her husband was cheating on her. She ran in front of the train. On foggy and cold nights, you see her reenact this event and hear her scream as the unseen train hits her.

DELAWARE
COUNTY

1116 W. North Street

Muncie: 1116 W. North St.

Footsteps stomp up the back steps. In 1993-96, great evil spirits was sensed by the residents. They felt as something wanted in, but needed to be invited.

403 W. Washington Street

Muncie: 403 W. Washington St.

A man haunts the top of the stairs. He is believed to be Charlie, a man that died of old age in the mid-1980s. He turns lights off and on and growls in the dining room. Students who live there report feeling a hit to the front room like a car or something large crashed into it, but nothing is amiss. It was a loud enough noise and physical shock that several items on a bookshelf fell off. One person who lived there, Angie, seemed to have a good rapport with Charlie; however he didn't like her roommates. Ray, one of the roommates, would find his pencils missing. He wouldn't go into the dining room because of Charlie. Another roommate didn't last long either. When Angie moved, she invited him to come with her, but he didn't. Her boyfriend, now husband, felt Charlie on the stairs as an "ice cold breeze". The second time it happened he said "Excuse me, Charlie" and went around him. Charlie appears as a shadow at times.

Ball State University

Muncie: The university website has an excellent interactive map for finding these locations on campus.

- Edwards Hall: The elevator randomly stops on the 9th floor.
- Elliot Hall: A WWII veteran, Will Schamberg, was disfigured by burning during the war. When he returned to school, he hung himself on the fourth floor of Elliott Hall. He stirs cool breezes and walks through the halls. Students report hearing a table moved to the area where Will hung himself. EVPs are caught in the building and orbs found in pictures taken in the area of Will's death.
- North Quad: Mysterious footsteps follow lone visitors.
- Phi Sigma Kappa House: Ask any Phi Sig and they can tell you all about "Leonard".
- Shively Hall: Doors mysteriously lock.
- Statue of Beneficence (Benny): cries blood tears when a virgin graduates
- Underground Tunnels: These tunnels were used for food transportation between Elliot and Johnson Halls. A rapist haunts the tunnels. They are no longer in use for safety reasons.

Ball State University- Christy Woods

Muncie: West of the Cooper Science building on University Blvd.

Named for Dr. Otto Christy, a former member of the science faculty, this 17 acre tract of land is open to the public during the day. Used for biology studies, students and visitors alike report many types of hauntings. A girl in torn, ragged clothing is seen on the south end of the woods. Her hair is ratted and she is very dirty. She has a wild look in her eye as if she's trying to escape something. When approached, she disappears. As this area is well known for the natural setting, it is only fitting that creatures are also included in the haunts. Visitors report a satyr romping in the late evening and sprites dance in the darkness of the nature preserve. Some students use the trails to jog. One woman distinctly remembers running one early morning and the fog was thick. She went slower than normal but as she came upon a curve in the trail, she heard a voice say "Be careful!" She said thank you and turned to see who it was, but no one was there. She ran forward and called out, but no one answered.

Carole's Curve
Daleville: 6400 W. CR 550S
(aka Dead Man's Curve)

A little girl haunted the attic of this home. She switches lights on and off. Her laughter is heard often and she likes to move items to different places. She told one resident to get out of the house. The same resident started to make arrangements to leave and then pets started to die.

Guthrie Park
Muncie: South of CR 2600 on CR 3900

A girl drowned in the pond and she is said to reenact her death in the now empty pond on a regular basis.

Hotel Roberts
Muncie: 420 S. High St.

This hotel was built in 1922 by George Roberts. He commissioned Charles W. Nichol to make a "showplace of Muncie". Virtually every part of this historic hotel is haunted. Shadow figures are seen throughout the building. Specific rooms are haunted by different spirits. Hotel Roberts is a gem of paranormal activity, if not a gem of beauty. The most notable experience is that of a woman who was either thrown or fell out the window of one of the rooms. She is heard whispering and was captured on video walking through the suite. Additionally, she likes to play with investigation equipment by clicking buttons and tapping microphones.

(Note: This hotel closed in late 2006 and at this time has no plans for reopening. It may be turned into senior living facilities.)

Madison's
Muncie: 2617 S. Madison St.

A restaurant once known as the SkyLine, the former owner lived upstairs and died. He haunts the place and turns light off and on. Also, he is heard walking through the restaurant.

Muncie Central High School
Muncie: 801 N. Walnut St.

A boy disappeared in Muncie and later his cleaned bones were found in the elevator shaft. A small pocket knife was found nearby. He is often seen walking through the halls at night.

Muncie Civic Theatre
Muncie: 216 E. Main St.

Visitors see a solid apparition of a woman in the middle of the center and left hand sections of the balcony. Visitors also report a feeling of being watched. The sewing and costume rooms are also host to ghosts- staff and visitors see apparitions of both men and women, doors slam and equipment has an odd way of relocating.

Oakhurst Gardens
Muncie: Minnetrista Cultural Center; 1200 North Minnetrista Parkway

The gardens are part of the Ball family legacy. From time to time, a girl and her grandmother are seen playing with a doll house.

Shoe Tree
Albany: Edgewater Road

While on a walk, an old man saw something in an oak tree. When he looked closer, the demon in the tree cut his throat, killing him. If you touch this tree, the demon will kill you and take your shoes, putting them in the tree as a trophy.

Rail Road Tracks
Oakville: East of CR S50W The tracks are in the middle of town.

Slaves supposedly built this track, although Indiana was not a slave state. Dark apparitions are seen on the empty train tracks.

Shanholtzer House
Eaton: 2065 E. Eden Rd.
(aka Emery House)

This 1850s home was the first house in the township. At one time it was a blacksmith shop, a hardware store and a general store. One of the owners saw three people moving a piano from the living room to the parlor- when they didn't own a piano. A translucent spirit, nicknamed Fred, has been seen in the kitchen (which was being remodeled at the time). It is known that one person died on the property when it was a general store, although the building is no longer on the property. A man shot his father because he heard his dad had been molesting school children. In the early 1800s, a cemetery was located down the road from the house. Early in the 1900s two sisters looked out the window and saw the front gate swinging back and forth for 20 minutes. This was very odd to them as it was a weighted gate and there was no wind at the time. The property is next to a school. The two sisters walked home one evening after an event and knew they weren't alone.

Springport Train Depot

Springport: East of SR 3 on CR W800N. The depot is at the corner of W. Main St. and the railroad tracks.

This train station is haunted by the ghost of the old train station master. He is seen walking through the building.

Union Cemetery

Eaton: Corner of CR N100E and CR E1000N (Eaton Wheeling Pike)

Upon entering the cemetery, the temperature drops. Visitors smell fresh flowers when none are present. This scent is prevalent in February and March. An invisible entity pushes people in the cemetery.

Witches Circle

Daleville: South of old SR 67 on Honey Creek Rd., drive until you make a 90 degree turn right, when you make another 90 degree turn left, you'll see a path that will go uphill slightly. You'll see a circle with several stones in it.

A transparent woman walks the area. Rumor has it that there is a circle of stones in the cemetery used by witches, which seems to be false. Other rumors include a shack that was the place where witches practiced. Investigators have been pushed and knocked to the ground by unseen forces. Psychics report that the spirits are scared. A little girl and her brother haunt the cemetery. Both were killed by their mother after she learned their father had been killed in battle.

FAYETTE COUNTY

Elmhurst

Connersville: South of Connersville on SR 121

(aka Old Elm Farm)

This mansion was built in 1831 by Congressman Oliver H. Smith and was occupied by other political leaders throughout the 1800s (including Caleb Blood Smith). Through this home's long history, it served the people of Fayette county, much as the original owner did. The house was part of the Underground Railroad as well as the Elmhurst School for Girls, and the Daum Annex, a sanatorium. It was also a military institute and a Masonic lodge.

Paranormal activity at this location include numerous orbs, EVPs of girls laughing, the sound of marching feet and singing. Small girls are seen skipping on the grass surrounding the building. Occasionally military buttons drop from no where in and around the building.

FOUNTAIN COUNTY

Historic Attica Hotel
Attica: 126 N. Perry St.

Built in the 1850s, the hotel was once host to Al Capone and Teddy Roosevelt. A former employee named Vida (Mennie) Foxworthy was murdered by a clock salesman who lived in one of the rooms. He took a .12 gauge and shot her in Room 21.

Vida touches people and calls out their names. Visitors hear scratching on the walls. The water in the showers turns off when you are still in the shower. A misty white woman seen in corridor. Visitors smell the scents of different flowers. Vida is considered a protective spirit as she has run off people who intend harm to the building. She also provides extra pillows for workmen.

Some visitors claim to see phantom lights, hear music and see ghostly images of people in and outside the hotel.

Mudlavia Spa
(See Warren County)

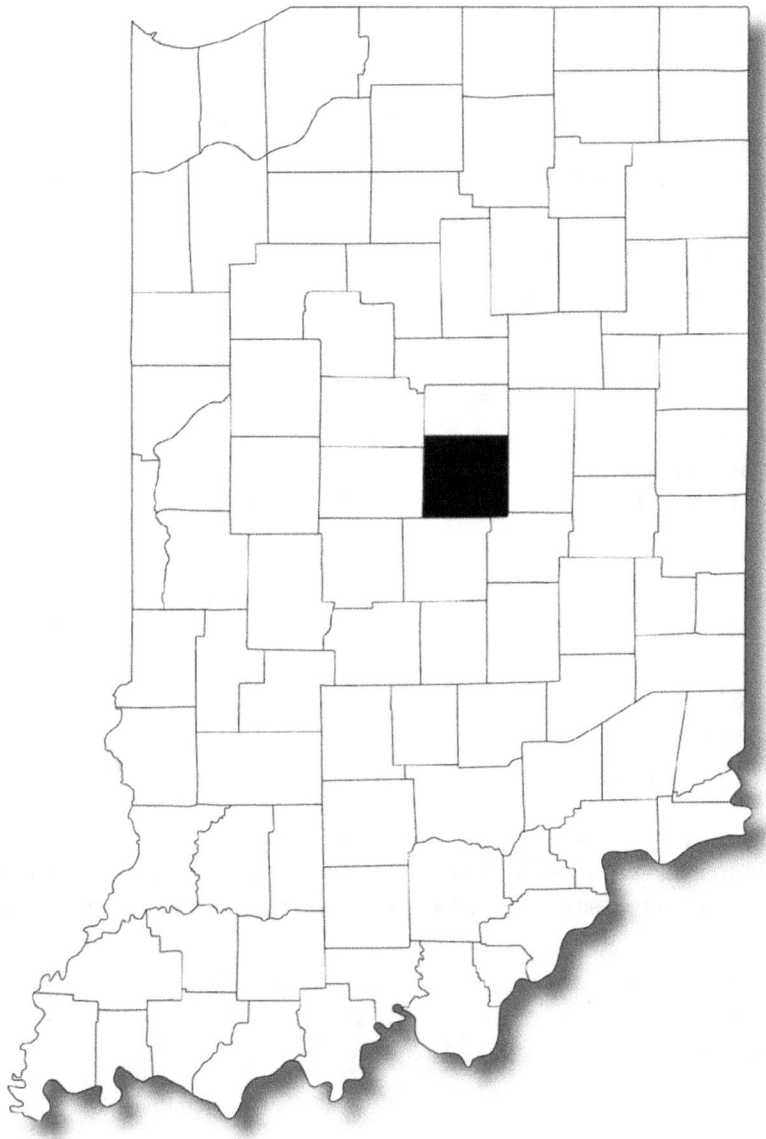

HAMILTON COUNTY

100 North Union Street

Westfield: 100 Union St.

(aka Old Bank)

Hank West, the old night watchman haunts this building. He turns up the heat to around 90 degrees. When people try to stop him, such as putting a lock box on the thermostat, he breaks the case and turns the heat up anyway. A woman and her daughter are seen in the building as well. They may be the same people seen in a building across the street.

101-103 South Union Street

Westfield: 101-103 N. Union 102-108 South Union St.

(aka Westfield Pharmacy and flowers)

The bell between the pharmacy and florist door rings on its own occasionally.

102-108 South Union Street

Westfield: 102-108 S. Union St.

(aka Jan's Village Pizza)

Visitors and staff report whispered names, phantom touches from unseen hands and lights malfunctioning. Orbs have also been reported on the second floor.

110 South Union Street

Westfield: 110 S. Union St.

(aka Keever's Hardware; Keltie's Restaurant)

When this restaurant was a hardware store (Keever's), a friendly ghost would help the owners fill orders. Many times they would have a list of items that would need to be pulled for customers and many times those items would mysteriously appear. When Keltie's was in business, muddy boot and dog paw prints appeared during closing and early in the morning.

112 East Main Street

Westfield: 112 E. Main St.

(aka Marlow's Restaurant)

Staff at this family owned business report hearing noises and having their apron strings pulled. Additionally, the back room is a hot bed of activity including having a dark figure pacing in the back room. Photos of the area show dark figures in pictures, although they were not visible at the time the photos were taken. The family believes the activity is from family members who used to work at the establishment and have passed on.

120 North Union Street
Westfield: 120 N Union St.

Former tenants report a mean old man turning on lights, throwing bottles, and hiding items. The smell of food not served in the building is also experienced.

130 Penn Street
Westfield: 130 Penn St.

(aka Old Town Hall)

Visitors and staff see shadows in the southern meeting room. The northern offices have a floating white mist. The ghost of a firefighter, Chad Hittle, was sensed a week after his death and his spirit is seen walking up and down the west stairs. Voices call out your name when you visit, especially around the restroom area. A group of tour guests saw a Quaker man in the southern meeting room during a tour. Another tour guest had his arm scratched by unseen fingernails.

132 W Main Street
Westfield: 132 W Main St.

(Razed)

This 1844 home was reputed as haunted as far back as 1932. An elderly woman lived in the house as a child and said the ghosts of her great grandparents inhabited the house. It was accepted as part of their life. Later others believe someone became unhappy with the disrepair that befell the house and noises throughout the day and night drove tenants out.

135 North Union Street
Westfield: 135 N. Union St.
(aka the Fern; the Stalker House)

Reported to have been a boarding house and a traveler's place of rest. Visitors heard moans and people walking throughout the house and out the front door. Before the building became The Fern, an older woman lived and died in the home.

136 East Main Street
Westfield: 136 E. Main St.

A burned man is seen in the upper story bathroom/former bedroom.

141 South Peru Street
Cicero: 141 S. Peru St.

Cold spots and mists are seen in home. At least three spirits of a man and two women haunt the home from top to bottom. One woman doesn't want anyone in the home, the one in the basement loves people in the home and the man on the stairs just goes about his business as in life. Still, according to one psychic, they were all happy that kids were in the home. In the coal room, reportedly a dead body was seen.

145 South Union Street
(aka Old Fire Station; Westfield Washington Historical Society Museum)
Westfield: 145 S. Union St.

This old fire station, now museum is home to the ghost of a firefighter named Bob Mikesell. Several staff and visitors feeling breezes as if someone was rapidly walking by them. EVPs recordings include "yes" in answer to the question, "Are you Bob?" and a booming laugh.

161st and Union Streets
Westfield: 161st and Union Sts.

Joggers see a Native American in buckskins walking along the road and surrounding trees.

1139 Cherry Street
Noblesville: 1139 Cherry St.

Residents report a Franciscan monk on the second floor. Strange whispers are heard in the attic.

14921 North Meridian Street
Westfield: 14921 N Meridian St.

Pots and pans fall to the floor at night when no one is in the kitchen. The music will turn on even when the system is in the off position. One woman was chased through the building by a cold breeze. When she got into the kitchen, she grabbed her purse and went out the back, pots and pans falling after her. For many years, a sign saying "Respect the Ghost" hung in the kitchen. Many people have quit because of the paranormal activity.

15513 South Union Street
Westfield: 15513 S. Union St.

Staff at the Cool Creek Park office hear a woman and her child in the building. A dirty looking man makes an occasional appearance. He seems to have worn some sort of eye protection but the rest of his face is black as if with soot. The park itself is haunted too. A woman had an encounter with a small boy who gave her an orange ball. She tried to find his mother, but he disappeared. Local lore states that a farmhouse speakeasy and a night club were once part of the area around the park.

17272 Futch Way
Westfield: 17272 Futch Way

Once farmland, the house is part of a subdivision. The midland trail runs behind the property. In the early 2000s, the home had a portal in one of the closets. Although not as active as when the owners first moved in and had small children, it still hosts a group of ghosts from time to time. The home has had no less than 15 ghosts including a vindictive old woman who was the great grandmother of one of the children, a perverted man who enjoyed watching people in the bathroom, and a 14 year old orphaned boy who used to ride the rails from town to town.

Now, the home has spirits that drift in and out as needed. Sometimes they need something communicated so someone who is still living. Other times they are ghosts that are brought home by the owner's paranormal and tour activities.

19037 Northbrook Circle
Westfield: 19037 Northbrook Circle

Former tenants saw a woman in a long skirt and long sleeved blouse in the northern most bedroom. Personal items went missing. The grounds have several type of trees and a good energy, however, there is a deep sadness in the house.

201 North Union Street
Westfield: 201 N Union St.

Currently a dermatology office, this house was once part of the Underground Railroad. Asa Bales had a barn at this location where fugitives were hidden in a basement. Parts of the barn remain in the back of the house.

People have witnessed objects moving and levitating. One witness saw the windows blow open with a stiff wind permeating the house. When she looked outside, not a branch was moving. A former owner had issues when her son would not sleep in his room because of the noise downstairs. She had her finger slammed in a door by unseen hands. She also received second degree burns from a cold stove.

273 South 8th Street
Noblesville: 273 S. 8th St.

This former home was reputed to be William Conner's home (because of the home's description) although most people believe that it could not be a William Conner's home because of the architecture. Most people believe that the home of Conner burned (as the location was notorious for fires) and that Leonard Wild built the house on what was Mayor

R.L. Wilson's homestead. Currently under new ownership, the former Accent Shop building is said to be haunted by a woman frequently seen in the NE window sitting at a sewing machine. Lights will mysteriously turn on when no one is around. According to some local visitors, the ghost may be that of Avalin Elizabeth Keeper, a retired employee of the Accent Shop.

301 East Main Street

Westfield: 301 E. Main St.

A phantom opens doors and closes them although no one is ever seen. A dark shadow is seen pacing the floors of the basement.

311 South Union Street

Westfield: 311 South St.

Shadow figures appear to visitors. A broom once flew across the room when it was a hair salon. On one ghost tour, a person took a pictures and three figures appeared in it.

319 South Street

Westfield: 319 South St.

A mean spirit of a middle aged man creates a hateful atmosphere.

323 South Union Street

Westfield: 323 S. Union St.

A little boy was ill one day and was lying on the couch downstairs. He wished he had his balloon and it floated down the stairs to him.

417 West Main Street
Westfield: 417 W. Main St.

(Razed)

This house has been home to many businesses but none stay long. Many people believe there is something "Wrong" with the building that goes beyond paranormal activity. Several former tenants believe a demon made its way into the house and now tries to take over people who enter. Currently, this house is slated to be demolished for US 31 reconstruction. Will the demon seek a new home?

421 South Union Street
Westfield: 421 S. Union St.
(aka Barker House)

Walking is heard in the old part of the upstairs. A cupboard opens on its own.

969 Keystone Way
Carmel: 969 Keystone Way
(Note: This is now an office building)

Illusions Restaurant was one of the most haunted restaurants. Strange footsteps are heard. A cane with a clown head on it mysteriously showed up after the owner killed himself in an upper office. Many of the furnishings were brought from Europe from funeral homes and castles. These items hold vibrations of the past. Shadow figures of men are seen in mirrors and several magicians' equipment failed to work. One storyteller reports her camera unable to function after a fully loaded 700 minute battery went dead in seconds. The women's restroom has a stall that will lock when the spirits are present and the water will turn off and on. The restaurant has many shadow figures that roam throughout and the alarm will go off at different times of the day and night.

Anti-Slavery Friends Cemetery
Westfield: Inside Asa Bales Park

The cemetery was attached to old Quaker meeting house of same name (no longer standing). Visitors see a wispy apparition of a woman in white, a solid color apparition of a Civil War solider, and orb masses.

145 W. Main St.
Atlanta: 145 W. Main St.

A translucent white woman with a bun and Gibson girl look watches out the window in the Spring.

Asa Bales Park
Westfield: Camilla Ct. and SR 32

Native Americans are seen walking through different areas of the park

Barley Island Brew Pub
Noblesville: 639 Conner St.

Suspected of being a former speakeasy as well as a buggy works, visitors report a little girl and a man in a hat, dusty books and work pants. Lights turn off and on. Staff and visitors have also been touched by unseen hands.

Fox Hollow Farms

Westfield: On the south side of 156th St. just west of the Monon Trail

Herbert Baumeister killed 4 known and several known victims, all men at this location. Tenants have elected to hold ghost hunts now and then. They say Herbert, who killed himself in Canada before he could be arrested, haunts the house. Herb is still aggressive, throwing items, yelling, and making threats. Residual hauntings occur in the guest house. In the woods where the bodies were dumped, visitors see a man in a hooded sweatshirt who seems to be running for his life. The pool, where much of the killing took place is also haunted. Dark figures and swimmers make appearances. Investigators see orbs, mists, and shadows.

Boys and Girls Club

Noblesville: 1448 Conner St.

Visitors and staff report children running through the old school. One visitor asked a child if she could help him and he disappeared before her eyes. At night, the lights turn off and on.

Commercial Building

Arcadia: SW corner of Main and East Streets

Bad vibes, dance hall, Victorian ceiling, people seen, radio heard, aliens seen.

East Union Cemetery

Atlanta: County Line Rd. and US 31

Cemetery has been investigated many times. Orbs and a mist that travels from north to south are experienced. Some investigators have been shoved and scratched in the cemetery.

Eck House

Cicero: 2811 Cumberland Rd.

Leonard Eck haunts this home. He built the house and has been seen by former family members who owned the home, visiting friends and by the current owners.

First Presbyterian Church

Noblesville: 1207 Conner St.

Visitors hear footsteps in the building. One boy witnessed an apparition moving from room to room. On staff member was surprised to see a woman in a long prairie skirt sitting in one of the basement rooms.

Hare House
Noblesville: 675 W. Walnut St.

This former funeral home is now home to a woman who walks up and down the stairs with a candelabra, a little boy named Charles, who runs around and plays tricks on people- and giggles. Finally, visitors report feeling sick, cold, and unhappy when in the upstairs area.

Harrell House
Noblesville: 399 N. 10th St.

The Harrell House was built by Dr. Samuel Harrell, who was a 7th son of a 7th son. He and his doctor brothers built the Harrell Hospital And Sanatorium (located at 148 N. 9th Street). Later the facility was sold and renamed Riverview. His Queen Anne home was built in 1898. The children's swings in the backyard move on their own even without wind. Other assorted ghosts roam throughout the home. Some visitors believe these ghosts are of the doctor and his patients. Others believe it is family and friends.

Heady Hollow
Fishers: 126th St. and Allisonville Rd.

A school house burned down and all the children died inside. On a foggy night, you see the children walking along the hollow. Sometimes you see them on the road and when you drive through them, they disappear like wisps of smoke.

(Note: Ron Baker's book on ghosts of Indiana mistakenly places this location on SR 13)

Hinkle Creek Church
Westfield: 21617 Hinkle Rd.

Visitors see white figures in the cemetery. Locals play midnight tag in the cemetery. One young boy spoke with the ghost children that inhabit the north side of the cemetery and said they have to wait 100 years before they can be reunited with their parents so until then, they like haunting and scaring people, especially children.

Holiday Drive Bridge
(aka Carmel Screaming Bridge)
Zionsville: Holiday Dr. off of US 421

A woman had a child outside of marriage. The father of the baby threw it in the woods. The mother went looking for the child and when she couldn't find it, she threw herself off the bridge and killed herself. Today she calls for the baby and weeps.

Klipsch Music Center

(aka Deer Creek; Verizon Wireless Music Center)

Noblesville: 12880 E. 146th St.

Formerly Deer Creek Music Center, this land used to be part of an old farm with a fieldstone house and fence. The original property had over 800 acres. The original stone house had a ghostly old woman who would click clack her tea cup and would fuss over bedding and curtains hanging strait. A black man (mentally challenged) was hung in the huge barn for supposedly raping a little white girl at the creek behind the property, but the little girl kept saying he was just her friend. When the barn still existed, you could still hear the sound of the rope in the third floor rafters of the barn.

Some visitors have suggested that Verizon might be haunted by Dave William's (musician from Drowning Pool) spirit, who died on his tour bus after playing Ozzfest in 2002.

Mill Creek Road

Westfield: Mill Creek Rd. and SR 32

The ghosts of a motorcycle wreck haunt the intersection.

Model Mill & Conference Center

Noblesville: 802 Mulberry St.

This building used to be home to the Model Mill, which showcased milling equipment and which did milling as well. Later it became Indiana Seed and now houses businesses and offices. Visitors and workers have seen apparitions and heard footsteps and voices. Investigators theorize that these occurrences could be due to the murder of a mill worker in the early 1900s.

Mount Pleasant Cemetery

Westfield: E. 236th St. and Anthony Rd.

No public access.

A dark caped figure chases people through the cemetery

Noblesville Antique Mall

Noblesville: 20 N. 9th St.

Formerly a Napa auto parts store, visitors report a woman in grey who either motions for people to follow her upstairs or motions for them to be quiet. In the south west corner of the basement, a creepy man stairs are shoppers.

Oak Road Bridge
Westfield: North of 151st St. on Oak Rd.

An unidentified white mist is frequently seen at dawn.

Oak Road Pond
Westfield: On Oak Rd., just south of South St. (171st St.)

Four children who died in the gravel pit pond try to lure you in. They appear as milk white translucent figures coming out of the pond. Some visitors say that when you're in the pond, they try to drag you under. Investigators captured a video of a rope swing (now gone) swaying during a still summer day.

Old Carmel Cemetery
Carmel: Northeast corner of Rangeline Road and Smokey Row (136th St.)
(aka Old Richland Friends Cemetery)

Visitors see a woman walking a dog and a man sitting under a tree. Mists exist in this cemetery when no other area is foggy.

Orphan's Home
Westfield: N. Union St. It is now two houses.

Ghost children still play in both locations. Giggling, toys rolling and disappearing, and small feet pattering are experienced.

Potters Bridge
Noblesville: 19401 N Allisonville Rd.

Built between 1870-1871 by Josiah Dufree, this bridge is the last of the covered bridges in Hamilton County. Closed to car traffic, it is part of a park. People hear hoof beats when no horse is around. They've also heard a man moaning when they were alone on the bridge.

Rhodes Hotel
Atlanta: 150 E Main St.
(aka Roads, Rhoades)

Information about Atlanta, Indiana is sketchy at best due to it being a small town and a firebug that destroyed much of the documentation in the 1990s. However, we do know that it was purchased in 1893 by Newton A. Rhoades for his wife, Clara. His father, Phillip was one of the earliest settlers in the area and was granted land "out west" after he fought in the Civil War.

In the early 1900s, a local newspaper touted the hotel as one of the best "east of the Mississippi". It was regarded as such because it boasted clean beds, tasty meals and a homey atmosphere. After the 1930s with bigger and better accommodations being built and the gas boom going bust, the hotel became a boarding house.

Other unsubstantiated legends peg this location as a speakeasy and a brothel. John Dillinger and Al Capone are also supposed to have visited the area.

In 2011, the house was purchased by a ghost hunting group for commercial investigations. The ghosts use flashlights to communicate to trigger questions. One ghost is supposed to be a pimp and another is supposed to be a hooker named Sarah. Dark shadows inhabit the upstairs rooms. One investigator was pushed down the attic stairs.

Riverside Cemetery
Noblesville: At the corner of Cherry and 5th Sts.

Founded in 1834, this cemetery has been somewhat neglected. After the flood of 1913, it became the "Negro cemetery", because if you put "them" in "there" no one would "bother them". Whatever.

People who visit loved ones feel a comforting hand on their shoulders. A Civil War soldier marches along the river fence line. A woman in white runs through the cemetery. On one ghost tour, the woman was seen by a group of 20 people. The author spoke to the woman and she disappeared. Despite all the pictures taken, she was not captured in a photo.

Riverwood
Riverwood (town)
Riverwood is bounded by White River, Riverwood Ave., and Riverwood Dr. (on the west side of IN 37).

Time warp experienced at this location. Rough cabins appeared and the people sitting by their cabins all looked mongoloid or inbred and would stare with vehemence at you. No one there was friendly and looked more like they would gut you and serve you up for dinner. There was one Victorian back on the river that was in good condition and it is reputed to come and go at will, as is the young long haired lass in a white dress with a green sash. The whole area around Riverwood seems disturbed and time damaged, it isn't so much a negative energy, as wrongness.

Screaming Bridge

(See Holiday Drive Bridge, Hamilton County)

Sheridan Historical Society
Sheridan: 308 S. Main St.

Grey figures seen. Items move. Footsteps heard.

Sheriff's Residence
(aka Hamilton County Historical Society)
Noblesville: Corner of Conner and 8th Streets

Staff and visitors hear footsteps downstairs and they hear doors opening and closing, yet when checked, nothing is amiss. Upstairs, a woman in turn of the 1900s clothing is seen. The jail cell on the first floor on the NE corner has a spirit that speaks or growls in your ear. The author was scratched in the guard area of the west cells after speaking with the ghost of a pimp. The apparition of a man in the juvenille cells was caught on camera after asking for any young men to show themselves. General feelings of dread are reported in the mens' cells.

Sleepy Hollow
Westfield: Grove of trees at the end of N Walnut St.

Strange shapes shift through the trees. Several people claim to have talked with and see pioneers from the town of Westfield.

Strawtown Cemetery
Strawtown: Essig Ave

The Shintapper family used to sell liquor to the Native Americans and once threw a drunken Native American on their 6ft long fire. When the other Native Americans heard of it, they plotted revenge. All the men in the area used to sharpen their weapons at the Shintappers. One day when a group of men were there, Native Americans exacted revenge, killing several white men and having several of their own men killed. Later that evening Shintapper went down the White River with his family and was never heard from again. Benjamin Fisher, was buried in Strawtown Cemetery very close to where he was killed.

Today, shadow people are seen on the ridge of the cemetery moving darkly through the property, even in daylight hours. EVP recordings include "help", "not me" and "go".

Strawtown Koteewi "Prairie" Park
Strawtown: 12308 E. Strawtown Ave.

In 1987 a set of heavy oak stairs went from the river to an old farm property near the park that a religious sect occupied and which contained a small gravesite of four adults and two children.

The park is a 750 acre home to archeological digs to learn about the ancient people who settled on the land. Footsteps are heard outside after dark. The unmarked Native American graves have mists that play over them at night. The path by the river has several translucent men running quickly down to the water.

Summit Lawn Cemetery
Westfield: On S Union across from Valley Farms Dr.

A girl in a school uniform makes people very unwelcome. Flashes of light play over the graves at night. People who live in the apartments across the street see white figures walking through the cemetery at night. Many people believe these are the people of the city still socializing.

Syd's Restaurant
Noblesville: 808 Logan St.

The longest running bar in Hamilton County, blond women have reported feeling a "cat-like" creature rubbing against their ankles. Staff report an old piano playing in the basement. The mannequin that sits in the front window changes position. Staff has taken to leaving a drink out for the ghost, called "Syd" in honor of a former owner.

Talbert House
(part of Christ United Methodist property)
Westfield: 318 N. Union St.

Harry Talbert, a former lumber baron built this house in the 1930s. Doors have open and closed on their own. Footsteps walk up and down the stairs. When they come in the next morning, the drink is gone.

Train Track Viaduct
Atlanta: North of town on E. Railroad St.

In the 1890s and later in the 1920s, men came running into town saying they saw a man waving a lantern. In the case of each occurrence, additional men went out to see for themselves and came back spouting stories of seeing the man walking toward them and disappearing when they tried to speak to him.

No known train accidents are known to have happened at this location, however, one theory is that this man died somewhere else on the line and is still on the job, making sure the train gets to its destination safely.

Union Bible College
Westfield: 434 S. Union St.

This former Quaker college (now a religious K-12 institution) houses a smaller version of the school now. Doors open and close on their own. Lights turn on in the library when no one is around. Visitors hear footsteps on the main staircase. In the adjoining hall, neighbors have the sound of music when the lights have been off and the hall closed.

Union Street
Westfield: Union St. just north of 161st St.

Native American in buckskins seen in this area and he will disappear in front of your eyes.

Vine Alley and Walnut Street
Westfield: Vine Alley between Cherry and Walnut Sts.

The town blacksmith's shop was two plats east of Walnut st. The McMullan funeral home was on the North west side of Walnut. Figures were seen traveling between the buildings. Both are gone now, but the occasional white mist persists.

The house on the south West corner of the intersection was owned by the White family who were early settlers of Hamilton County. Former owners claimed one of the White family members would help her make business decisions.

Walton House
Atlanta: 100 East Main Street

This house was built by Asher Walton in 1868 across from his mercantile store and his successful bank. It has changed hands over the years and at one time was a bed and breakfast. Visitors and staff report a persistent dark shadow that follows them down the main staircase.

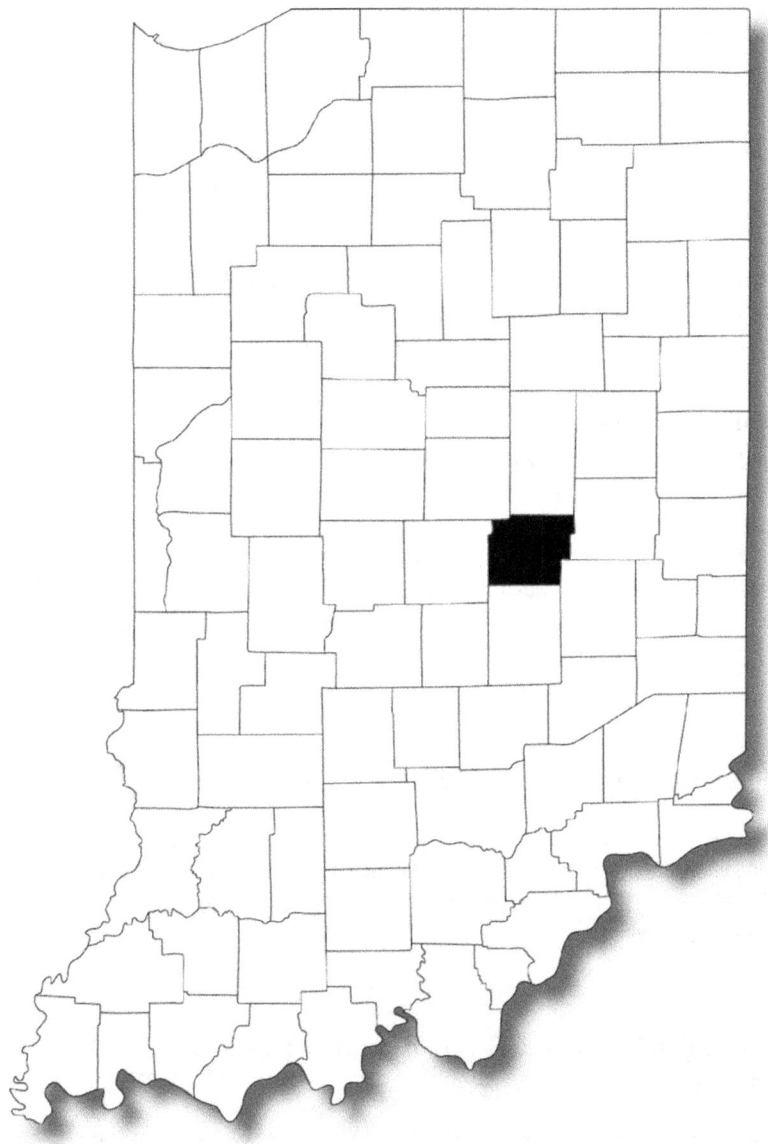

HANCOCK COUNTY

11608 E Washington Street

Cumberland: 11608 E Washington St.

At Clippty Do Dawg, a pet grooming business, items fall off shelves, unseen people talk, dogs growl and bark.

During one paranormal incident, the owner was grooming a dog. She saw a bottle fly off table and land in doorway. Another bottle flew through a room when the owner was meeting with a client. Shadow people stalk and watch employees and the animals.

A dog being boarded somehow escaped from his cage. In the morning the staff found the light on and the cage he was in locked. Paranormal investigators caught orbs and a mist from the ceiling. When the owners used dowsing rods, they discovered the ghost's name was Charles, which matched the owners name from the 1800s.

Abraham Lincoln Ghost Train

Greenfield: Seen on April 30th on Greenfield on tracks that are south of US 40 between midnight and 7am

People report seeing the Lincoln ghost train which carried his body through Indiana. (Lincoln's ghost is probably the most transient spirit having been seen at several places within Indiana, at the White House, and in Springfield, IL. The legend has identified two trains. The first has several black crepe draped cars and the other is just a flatbed car with the casket lying on top.

Cry Baby Bridge

Milners Corner: Thomas Rd. between CR E950N and CR E1000N

Depending on the story, this is where a woman died with her baby or where a baby died in a car crash. In one version of the story, the baby wasn't found when the police investigated. In another version, the baby was found half eaten by dogs (sometimes still crying, but it died later). Still another version said the mother buried it alive. In any of these versions, if you go across the bridge you can hear crying.

Hays Cemetery

Milners Corner: Thomas Rd. between CR E950N and CR E900N
(aka Main Street Graveyard)

Some people believe a girl who made a pact with the devil is buried here. Other visitors have seen orbs, mysterious figures and even devilish beings. Some people have reportedly chased through the cemetery by specters ranging from an old man to a younger man with a hatchet.

McCray Cemetery
Wilkinson: Off SR 109 and CR N1000E

Residual haunters abound in this cemetery. Many apparitions have been seen at the same time.

Old Fair Grounds
Greenfield: SW corner of Market and Third Sts.

James Keener was the lamplighter of Carthage and an African-American Civil War veteran. In 1875 James' son Billy was lynched as a rapist. Billy's last words were "Men, you are doing a great wrong." People came to view "the rapists" body and he was buried in the Greenfield Potter's field. James was outraged and supposedly said "I hope I live to see all of them dead." Three of the men who were part of the lynch mob met bad ends. One became terminally ill, yelling for people to "get that man away from me". Another was killed in an explosion, and the other was killed in a car crash. Billy's innocence was never proven, although later the woman who accused him recanted.

Today, because of the great wrong done at the lynching site at the old fair grounds, people have reported feeling a sense of dread and malice.

The Plantation Club
McCordsville: CR 700W and Pendleton Pike
(aka Casio's; razed)

A speakeasy in the 1930s and a place for gangsters for longer than that, the Plantation Club saw its fair share of action. It had bulletproof panels, a foot thick steel cash door and tunnels for quick getaways. Known for gambling and women, several cabins were provided in back of the bar for extra entertainment. After one woman known for wearing blue was killed, she was seen roaming the cabins.

A woman was killed by her jealous husband in the club's cloakroom. From that time forward, that room had one area that was extremely cold. One employee would hear knocks on the door, but no one would be there.

In its last incarnation, the speakeasy was known as Casio's. The former owners Mike and Donni Nickerson couldn't save it from the wrecking ball and the establishment was razed.

Now it is a wider road and a closed driving range. Avid ghost fans still go by to take pictures. They capture many orbs. One has to wonder if the patrons of the driving range were touched by the woman in blue.

Weston Village Apartments
Greenfield: 424 Roosevelt Dr.

A woman saw a one-eyed monster in her bedroom. Others have seen the ghosts of a man in tattered clothing, and a woman with a burned face. Another ghostly woman gently blows in the ears of the males in this apartment complex.

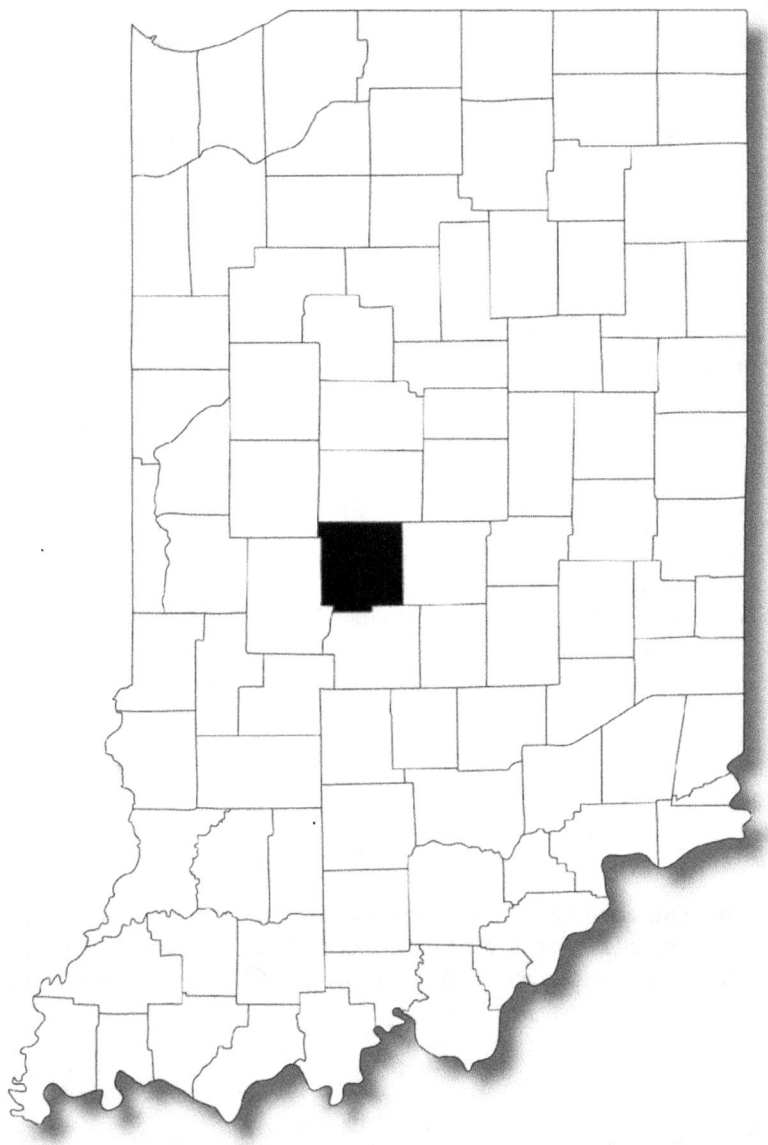

HENDRICKS
COUNTY

Creature from Hell
Danville: Land west of Danville

Two friends were rabbit hunting in 1883 and went into the forest to the west of Danville. They were chased by a creature resembling a horse with blue flame eyes. Other people said it had zebra-like features. Others believed it had a forked tongue and snakes for a tail.

Danville (town)
Danville

Charlie O. Williams is reported to haunt the area. Police Officer William Wright has a picture from October 18, 2002 after a car accident that occurred at Clinton and Maples Streets. Charlie is in the picture in the middle of the fog. He is also heard whistling and jingling coins- as he did in life.

Davee Home
Danville: 3527 Cartersburg Rd.

Once a popular mineral springs resort that operated into the early 1900s, this house is a home to multiple spirits. A girl in a blue dress runs around the yard. She is also known to turn lights on and unlatch a gate. Conversations from disembodied voices are heard around the pool. A ghost is seen in the laundry room of the home, apparently as surprised to see visitors as the visitors are to see them. One of the upstairs rooms is host to ghost voices. Orbs have been seen as well.

Haunted Bridge
Avon: CR 625E, just south of US 36
(aka Danville Bridge, aka White Lick Creek Bridge)

An Irishman, Dad Jones, fell into the wet cement and drowned in one of the supports when the bridge was built. He is encased in the bridge. A woman jumped off a train that was passing over the bridge. Screams, moans and whispering are heard. The apparition of a man is also seen and tapping can be heard from the bridge (supposedly the man tapping to get out).

Haunted Bridge
Danville: South of US 36 to the east of Shady Lane on East Broadway.

Although this location is often confused with the Avon Bridge and vice versa, another version of the story goes that a woman jumped with a baby off the bridge because she was unwed and felt she had no choice. Now, hauntings range from the appearance of the woman, a crying baby, a woman that will attempt to push you off the bridge.

Hummel Park
Plainfield: 1500 South Center St.

By the bridge over the river on the west side of the park, a woman holds a child and screams, terrifying visitors.

Maplewood
Around Maplewood

On November 1, 1883 the Danville Republican reported that a creature with the head of a horse "as large as a pork barrel" was seen in the area. The creature's six inch long and wide eyes shot light from them. The hair on the beast writhed like black snakes. Its zebra like body was covered in feathers all the colors of the rainbow. The wings were 12ft long and its tongue spit fire, which killed anything within six feet of it. It also has three feet long horns. When it climbs trees, the tree instantly withers and dies.

Royal Theatre
Danville: 59 S. Washington St.

A middle aged couple is seen in the theater. Noises are heard in projection booth and restrooms. Lights turn off and on. Light bulbs malfunction. Sometimes the spirits laugh at you or call your name.

HENRY
COUNTY

Community Corrections
New Castle: 100 Van Nuys Rd.

Disembodied voices are heard throughout the facility.

Guyer Opera House
Lewisville: 110 W. Main St.

During a popular Wild West gun show, a little boy was killed by a ricocheting bullet. The same year, the owner OK Guyer died. His funeral was held in the opera house.

Dressing room lights mysteriously turn on, off and burn out. Sometimes the lights will turn on, one by one and turn off the same way. Odd loud noises come from the back of the auditorium and temperature changes (hot and cold) are common. The auditorium doors open and close by unseen hands. The light booth also experiences drops in temperature. Shadow and transparent figures are seen throughout the building, especially on stage and in the dressing rooms.

Monkey Jack Bridge
New Castle: S. of S. Greensboro Pike on CR S225W

A couple had car trouble. He went for help. She stayed. The wind started and the rain came. After, she hard a scratching. Thinking it was her boyfriend,, she got out and found him with a knife in his back, his throat cut and hanging from a tree. The scratching was his fingernails on the roof of the car. If lovers go there, they will hear this too.

Pest House
Knightstown: SR 109 as you enter Knightstown. It is a private home and a great example of red brick Victorian Empire style architecture with its tower and dormer windows.
(aka Morgan House)

Originally, this home was built by Charles Dayton Morgan who was a wealthy banker, lawyer and state representative. In the 1920s this building was used to quarantine victims with contagious diseases and long term issues such as TB. The death rate was very high. Even before that, Knightstown had its share of trouble with the 1902 small pox epidemic. The building is haunted by people who died in the building.
The site of the quarantine station is very active, with nurses and patients walking next to it. A lady in a black dress haunts the building. Some people have witnessed furniture moving on its own across the floor. One ghost will open the door to visitors and tell them no one is home.

Train Depot
Springport: CR E800N West of IN 3

A young man in a suit is seen walking through the building.

HOWARD COUNTY

208 E. Mulberry Street

Kokomo: 208 E. Mulberry St.

(aka Old Jacob's Funeral Home)

This location is rumored to have been a Sears and Roebuck store and an African-American funeral home. In 1901 it was known as the Smith and Keller Funeral Parlor, later to become Smith and Hoff. In 1919 it became known as Jacob's Funeral Home. Orbs drift through the funeral home. Black shadows walk through the building and basement. Some people believe it smells of decomposing bodies. A black fog is said to seep through the building. Screams have been heard. Shadow figures are seen. Many items at the funeral home seem to hold paranormal properties. Water turns on and off, as do lights. Visitors hear footsteps throughout the building.

3510 Southlea Drive

Kokomo: 3510 Southlea Dr.

Doors open, and people hear cups moving around. Wind would move through the home like a whisper. The front door opens and closes, unlocking for no reason. Cold spots are felt even on warm days. A cold beer can was found one morning on the stove when no one had put it there. Doors would open, but with the lock set in locked position. Families seem to move out quickly.

Adams Mill

(See Benton County)

Carter Street (50 N) and County Road 400 East

Kokomo: North east corner of Carter St. and CR 400E

A man and his mother lived together. She died and haunted the house. Her son moved because he couldn't handle living with the paranormal. Transparent figures seen moving within the house. Orbs are seen and strange taps are heard on cars.

County Roads 600 East and 500 North

Kokomo: CR 600E and CR 500N

(Note: Home and barn are gone. Another house occupies the spot.)

The house contained a locked room in which an entity was released in 1972. The day it was released a young man, Bob, who was about to leave for Vietnam, rifled through the historic belongings in the room. As he went to bed that night, someone yelled, "Keep that door locked!" Bob's wife Carolyn of a woman in a long skirt was saw and heard. An apparition of a young girl looking out the front door has also been witnessed; footsteps were heard all over the house. Some of the issues are attributed to a man who hung himself in the old barn.

Ferrell House
Plevna: Razed

Crops will not grow where the house and barn used to be. A woman hung herself in the barn and her ghost was often seen swinging from a rope.

Gateway Gardens
Kokomo: 800 E. Hoffer St.
(aka Garden Square Apartments)

Rumored to have been built on an old graveyard, some people believe that not everyone was removed and relocated. Legs without bodies walk the area, and teardrops fall from the ceilings.

The C row apartments have the most activity. In apartment C-1, demons were said to influence and possess people living in the apartment. C-3 reports telephones ringing with no one on the line or voices that sound as though they are coming from a long distance and seem to come mainly from dead family and friends. C-11 reports feelings of being watched as well as seeing shadow people.

Disembodied legs and legs in boots are seen frequently. People have reported being locked in the apartment without provocation. C-13 has had apparitions of people in different time periods from mid 1800s to the early 1900s. Other children who grew up in this apartment reported having talked with spirits about their lives. Some of the spirits wanted the children to "come with them".

In F-16 instances of demons influencing children have been reported. Legend has it that a son pushed his mother down the stairs in this apartment and broke her neck.

Hopewell Cemetery
Kokomo: On Van Sickle Rd. (CR 400E) just north of Carter St. (CR E50N). Once on Van Sickle Rd., take the first left. Somewhat overgrown.

Transparent apparitions walk through the cemetery. Apparitions of a small boy are seen. Sometimes he is playing with an airplane and other times he's crying.

Jerome Cemetery
Greentown: CR150S and CR1000E

A shadow figure in a black cape is seen in the cemetery with two dogs. Fogs and mists appear at will.

Kokomo Hum
Kokomo

Almost 100 residents in Kokomo have reported feeling ill and have sought medical treatment for headaches, joint pain and other symptoms they attribute to "the Kokomo hum". Since residents have reported a hum that only can be heard in certain areas. Many people believe that it is caused by industrial equipment, mining, or factories outside Kokomo. The city of Kokomo hired a firm, Acentech Inc., to investigate and they alleviated the issue somewhat by finding an air compressor at the Hayes International plant. Still, other people still believe the noise is extraterrestrial in nature.

Satan's Church and Prairieville Cemetery
Russiaville: CR W650N between CR N1100W and SR 26

This cemetery next to church, boasts glowing red eyes, shapeless mists and whispers. Growling and mysterious voices are heard throughout. It is claimed that a cult used the church for rituals.

Seiberling Mansion
Kokomo: 1200 W. Sycamore St.
(aka Howard County Museum)

Some people see a solid figure of a woman seen in a rocking chair. The reflection of a mannequin that had been moved to a different floor was seen in a first floor mirror immediately after it has been moved. The basement seems to be a hotbed of activity filled entities and lights mysteriously going out without warning.

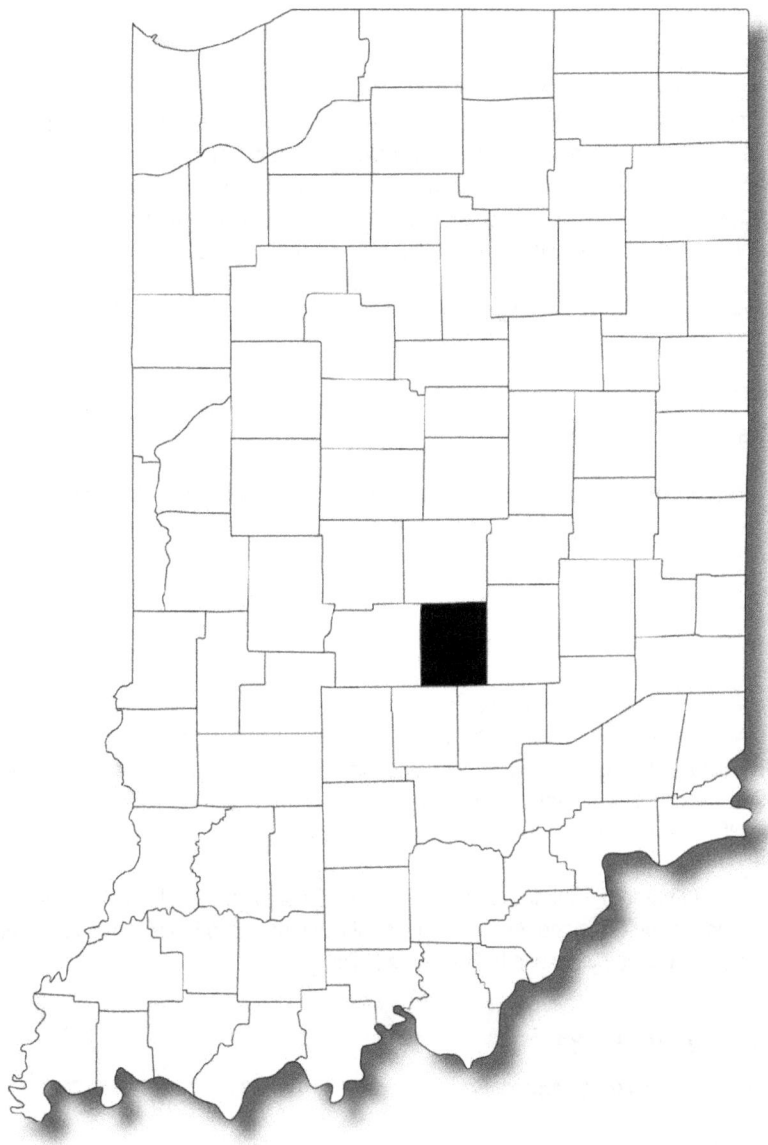

JOHNSON COUNTY

Atterbury Job Corps Center
Edinburgh: Hospital Rd.

Footsteps are heard frequently on the campus when no one is around. Yellow glowing eyes are seen in the woods. A woman holding her head in her hands walks around. By the field house, a scarred man walks and talks to himself. WWII soldiers walk through the building. In one dorm a clock flew off the wall. In the Rosa Parks dorm, three women from the Civil War era walk through the dorm. The cemetery on the property is a hotbed for orbs. The apparition of a small boy talks with you about his red truck. A discussion between a woman and a man can be heard, although it is unclear what they are saying. Legend also places the area as a Native American burial ground and Native Americans have also been seen as well. In the theater, a man in black sits in a chair. He is believed to be the same man in the woods. Sometimes he whistles. People describe feelings of sickness in different areas.

First Christian Church
Edinburgh: 306 S. Walnut St.

Orbs and a grey mist have been captured at this location. A transparent stooped old man who shuffles slowly is seen entering the building.

Franklin College
Franklin: 101 Branigin Boulevard

- Bryan Hall: In the early 1980s, a fire destroyed much of this building, a student burned to death. Today students and staff smell burning flesh and fire to the point that classes have been cancelled. Screams are also heard. Legend has it that an older girl killed a younger one, dismembered her, and put her in a wall. She was found in the wall of the second floor during summer break. She is heard beating against the wall and crying. A professor hung himself in the attic and the rope is supposed to still be in place. The door to the 4th floor opens even if it's locked.
- Old Main Theatre: It is haunted by Charlie. Supposedly a French student hung himself in the theater. One student had a person appear on the piano. Another student playing the piano heard someone scream, "GET OUT!" People have been touched by unseen hands in this building.

Greenwood Cemetery and US 31
Greenwood: West of US 31 north of Main St.

A girl in white walking by the road will get in and ask to be taken home. Before she can tell you, she disappears. Other times, they say she runs through Greenwood Cemetery.

Henderson Cemetery
Greenwood: CR W200N and CR N575W

(no public access)

Locals believe the Grim Reaper himself haunts this cemetery in hopes to find new victims. People hear footsteps when no one is around and a shadow figure wearing a tattered cape is seen gliding through the cemetery during both night and day. Strange figures that dance at the corner of visitors' eyes are reported

Historic Artcraft Theatre
Franklin: 57 N. Main St.

This 600 seat theater opened in 1922 as a vaudeville and silent movie theater. Below the stage are the original dressing rooms. Perfume is smelled and shadow figures are seen in the third and eighth rows of the theatre. Seats lower and rise at will. EVPs have also been captured.

Main Cemetery
Franklin: On South St. across from Tearman Hotel

Many experience feeling of discomfort are felt. Recently EVPs of a woman with static over her voice said that she wanted to get out. Another EVP caught a woman asking "what am I supposed to do?"

Nicholson Home
Greenwood: Moved from Mills and Mann Roads to Southport and Mann Roads in 1997.
(aka Rand Home)

David Nicholson, a contractor for the Marion County Courthouse, built this home from 1870 to 1876. The Rand family owned the home from the early 1900s until the mid 1960s. Part of the home's legend states that it was once used as a boarding house and someone committed suicide by hanging in the middle upstairs bedroom. In 1997 it was moved by the Indiana Historic Landmarks Foundation to its current location. The day it was scheduled to move, one of the trucks carrying half the home wouldn't start. In retrospect, some people speculate that the home didn't want to be moved after all. Locals, who were quite interested in the move told stories of a child accidently shot by hunters nearby. Her spirit and those of a nearby cemetery haunted the home. Another story is that a little girl broke her neck after falling from the home's second-story balcony. An Indianapolis Star photographer took a picture of the home in which a little girl was peering out from an upper window. The photo is now all over the Internet.

Investigators have reported odd EMF readings in the building, which is now a private home.

Podunk

Bargersville: Go south on SR 135 and turn right on Division Rd, which becomes a narrow road, eventually turns into a twisting narrow road. Eventually the road will become Podock. When you reach Podock and Dillman Road, you've reached Podunk.

(See also Nashville, Brown Co.)

A baby crawls on the road and sometimes laughs and cries. Visitors feel emotional outburts. Some have been pushed and scratched. A story claims a phantom truck follows motorists. One version of the stories at this location includes a phantom truck that will follow you. Many people have reportedly seen this truck and lights that appear and disappear just as quickly. Investigators have seen strange mists and half apparitions.

Toner Maley House

Edinburgh: 606 E. Main Cross St.

This bed and breakfast is full of elegance and the royal treatment. From pillow-top mattresses, candlelight breakfasts and plush sheets, this location is not only a pleasure to stay in but a wonderful place for a haunting.

Spirits like to spend time in the library. A woman and a man have both been seen reading and looking at books. As you approach them, they smile and disappear. The woman is in an elegant Victorian dress with upswept hair. The man, who has mutton chop sideburns, sits in a chair, smoking a pipe. A young woman in early 1900 clothing and a suffragette hat walks down the stairs and slams the front door.

Willard Restaurant

Franklin: 99 N. Main St.

Built in 1860 as a hotel it was later sold to a prohibitionist, Eliza Willard. Many visitors believe that she haunts the establishment in an effort preven drinking and other vices. Several people report having tried to light cigarettes only to have their matches and lighters extinguished with a puff of wind. People felt as if they were watched. The scent of lavender and gardenias lingers in the air. Other visitors report a presence in the woman's restroom. Several unexplained photos have been taken and apparitions have been seen. EVPs of a woman's voice have also been caught by investigators.

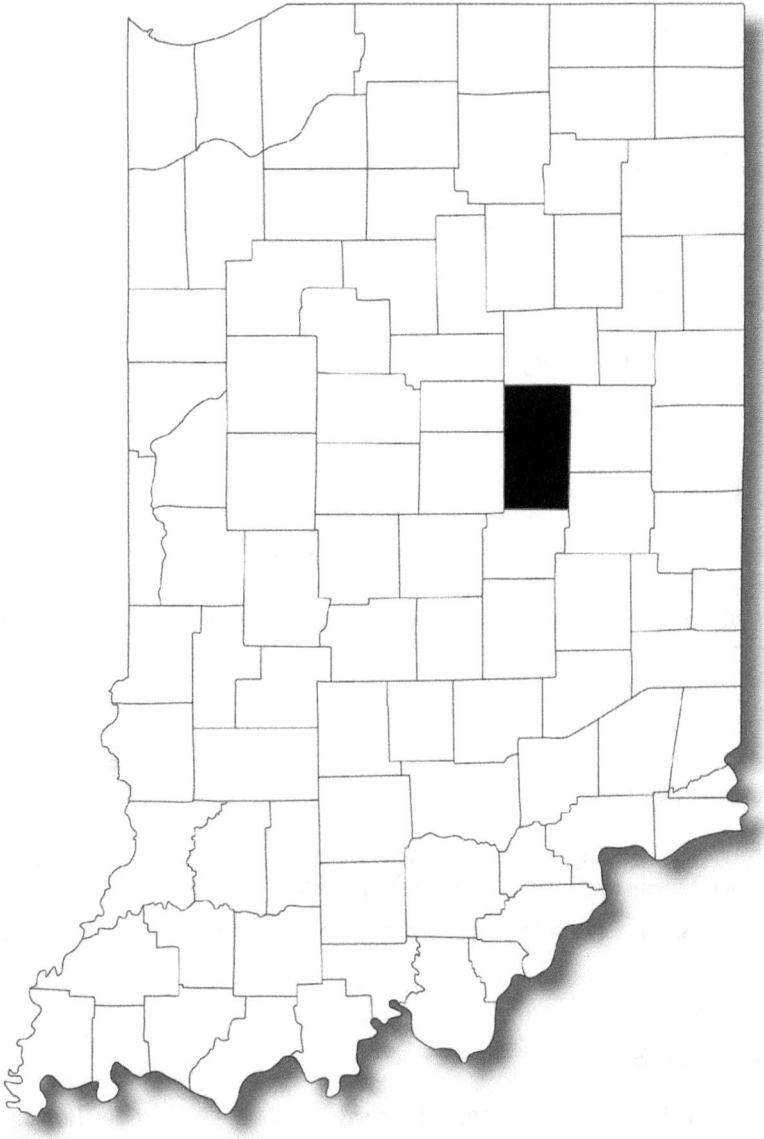

MADISON COUNTY

107 E. Pierce Street
Alexandria: 107 E Pierce St

A girl in overalls is seen in the house. She pulls pranks on people such as pulling their arms or touching their hands in the kitchen. She has also been seen in the early morning in the living room, sitting in a rocking chair. The girl visited one person in a dream and indicated there was a diamond under the floor boards of one of the bedrooms.

1118 Meridian Street
Anderson: 1118 Meridian Street

This building has the ghost of a crying woman in early 1900s clothing. Nothing more is known about the woman.

1412 Main Street
Elwood: 1412 Main St

This 1880s building has been home to many businesses. In the 1940s the front was remodeled for a nightclub. iIt is believed during this time that a fight broke out and two men killed each other over a woman named Lottie, who was one of several taxi dancers at the night club. A former owner remembers doing some renovations between tenants and witnessed a man chasing another through the back hallway and down the stairs. Lights are still seen in the building today and over the last few years, the building has stood more empty than used.

206 Vineyard Street
Anderson: 206 Vineyard Street

Formerly a boarding house, religious publishing house, this home is full of playful spirits who never make a physical appearance. One that rushes out the front door, and another likes to visit folks in the bathroom. Another likes to walks down the stairs. It is believed these spirits are those of people who stayed at the home while it was a boarding house.

709-711 Meridian Street
Anderson: 709-711 Meridian St.

Chief Anderson has been sighted on the rooftop of buildings in the area. It used to be the Meridian Hotel, across from the old police station.

6451 W. 300 South
Anderson: 6451 W 300 S (53rd St.)

Cory Clark and her daughter Jenna were killed here a few years ago. They were killed by Frederick Baer who randomly picked them. He first slit Cory's throat and then chasing 4 year old Jenna down and slitting her throat as well. He returned to Cory to rape her but was unable to complete the act.

Today, the duplex is haunted by the sound of running footsteps and piercing screams. The neighboring duplexes along the road are put on the real estate market often.

1218 W. 6th Street
Anderson: 1218 W. 6th Street

A variety of ghosts have been seen and felt in the house. Once home to suffragists, the building has several ghosts. A woman is seen in the upper hallway, seemingly upset that her view to the oval window (now covered by vinyl siding) is blocked. Additionally, an older woman who used to live in the west side (when it was apartments) can be heard talking. Phantom steps walk up stairs that no longer exist.

700 W and 300S
Anderson: SW corner

One could never guess from the outside that this bungalo-eque house was once in part a one room school house. Throughout the house ghosts have been seen, felt and heard. In the upstairs bathroom, the apparition of a child is seen. In the schoolroom, a bodiless pair of boots pace in front of the fireplace. Phantom footsteps are heard up and down the stairs. A caped man was seen throughout the 1970s and 1980s in the house. 30 years after these events, he was seen in the barn. A demonic entity scuttles about the downstairs late at night and an incubus took advantage of a young woman in one of the upstairs bedrooms.

Airport Rd. Bridge
Elwood: W 1000 N and SR 37

In 1965, Joseph Lila killed himself at 8pm on this bridge by shooting himself in the mouth. He reenacts this event on the anniversary of his death- May 24.

Anderson High School
Anderson: 4610 Madison Ave.

A teenage girl from the 1960s killed herself when she found that a boy she liked wasn't going to take her to a dance as promised. She is seen hanging in the old auditorium (now classrooms) and she walks through the new part of the school (formerly part of the outdoor area).

(Note: Anderson High School was originally located by the WigWam on Lincoln St. In the 1990s, Anderson High School was relocated in the Madison Heights High School on the south side of Anderson. Long live the MHHS Pirates- You may have jackhammered our beloved mascot but Pirates never die!)

Arby's Restaurant

Anderson: 2820 Broadway St.

A big man sits in the lobby and frequents the men's restroom, opening the door with unseen hands. Employees report seeing him walking through the kitchen after hours.

Aqua Gardens

Anderson: Aqua Gardens (now an activity center for Shadyside park). The area in which a girl died is now owned by Aqua Marine of Anderson located at 1115 Alexandria Pike. *(aka Activity Center for Shadyside Park)*

Aqua Gardens was purchased by the city of Anderson in 1970 and renamed Shadyside Recreation Center. In the 1960's some teenagers coupled up and decided to have an evening party at the swim beach. They had a small fire, a few beers, and marshmallows to roast. Things turned for the worst when everyone decided to go skinny dipping. Amy Chapman couldn't swim, but got in the water with everyone else. It was dark and no one could see very well. Amy must have stepped in a hole or into deeper water and drowned while everyone else was splashing and yelling. No one heard her cries for help. At daybreak, her body was found floating.

For years afterwards Aqua Gardens was closed except for a trail that bordered the former swim beach. Locals knew the unfortunate girl roamed the area. Children were cautioned about going back to Aqua Gardens.

If anyone is there after dark, she is seen on the shore, wet and wearing mossy seaweed. She warns other swimmers to not venture out very far. Sometimes she is seen floating on top of the water late at night to keep others from skinny dipping and drowning.

Bethel Pike Bridge
Alexandria: W 1100 N east of Orestes Rd

On June 13, 1955, five men on this bridge died after it collapsed. Two cars hit head on and were thrown into the water. The people in the car were between the ages of 18 and 23. You can sometimes hear the reenactment of the event, and can hear the men groaning and calling for help.

Bickels Cafe
Anderson: 21 W 8th St.

This location suffered an all-day fire on August 30, 1878 during a fireman's strike. Some non-striking fighters attempted to gain control, but it was insufficient. Other firefighters were called in. The strikers refused to help and tried to prevent anyone from fighting the fire. The blaze destroyed over 10 businesses. A man was found dead in this building's stairwell after the fire was out. Immediately a parking lot was made over this artificial grave.

Since the fire, visitors have smelled smoke in the building. Footsteps are heard. The apparition of a man, believed to be the man who perished in the fire, is seen walking though the building at night.

Bocco Cemetery

Anderson: West side of CR100E, between CR350S and CR400S

It is named after Issac Bucco (aka Bocco), who donated the land for the cemetery. Orbs and an apparition of a woman are reported in the south west corner of the cemetery.

Bronnenberg Home

Anderson: SR32 to Rangeline Rd. onto E 100 N (Lindberg Rd). *Razed.*

The Lindberg home was originally a family home, which later turned into an orphanage Today it has all but disappeared. The home reverted to its former grandeur when visitors entered the home. When the wind blew, the dust swirled around unseen figures.

Note: This home has since been razed and the land where the house once stood is now the Bronnenberg Youth Center.

Buck Creek Bridge

Anderson: East of Rangeline Rd on E CR450N Access it east of N CR1000W on E450N. *(aka Activity Center for Shadyside Park)*

Built in 1910 and restored in 1984. Visitors report seeing a noose with a body swinging from the bridge.

Camp Chesterfield

Chesterfield: North of SR32 on Washington St. *(aka Spook Camp)*

In this peaceful place, ghostly figures are said to walk freely on the grounds. Many voices are heard when no one is around. In the past, Harry Houdini proved some of the spiritualist techniques used in the early 1900s were fake. Today, this serene area is home to a retreat-type atmosphere, public events and a religious shrine. A small child haunts the woods. Both the Western and Sunflower Hotels have reported activity. People hear footsteps and conversation when no one is present.

One group of people who decided to plan a trip had a terrifying dream the night before. All of them dreamed that spirits from the camp were hovering over them and wanted to take them with them. Needless to say, they never went.

(Note: The Sunflower Hotel is not open for overnight stays.)

Chesterfield Christian Church
Chesterfield: 207 E. Plum St.

A man was found dead in the boiler room in the 1940s. His death was never solved. Today lights flicker off and on. Doors open and close by unseen hands. Mysterious handprints on windows and mirrors appear without cause.

Destroyed Cemetery
Alexandria: Southeast corner of Harrison and 4th Streets (next to Alexandria School of Scientific Theraputics)

This destroyed graveyard is now a parking lot with a small marker commemorating the location. History doesn't indicate if the bodies were actually moved when the area was paved. From earliest times, this spot has been home to ghost stories. Originally a graveyard, then a church were built upon it. However, when girls were kidnapped, never to be found again, it was decided it was too far out and the Native Americans were too much of a threat. The girls were said to haunt the area.

Eventually, the land reclaimed the burial ground. One account states that when the storms rolled in and the wheat was high, the graveyard looked like spirits were rising from their graves (although one ghost was proven to be crows). The ghost travels through town often visiting Chaplain Cemetery, Beulah Park and has also been seen on Berry, Black and Monroe Streets.

Dicky Road
Anderson: Dickey Road, just west of Dr. Martin Luther King Blvd.

(aka W 57th Street)

The railroad tracks on this road have long been a source of legend. Even before Anderson Memorial Park Cemetery was established, a misty, dark apparition of a funeral procession was seen near the railroad tracks heading south to north.

Elder House
Alexandria: Right side of Park Ave, just north of E 1000 N

Strange lights can be seen at night, but no one or nothing is found.

Elwood Opera House
Elwood: 202 South Anderson Street

Constructed in 1887, this opera house was an all-purpose. After it discontinued opera in 1905, the Masons used dthe building and it had several professional offices. The "blue room" was used by the Masons and seems to be a hotbed of paranormal activity. Shadow figures race from place to place in the building. Doors open and close randomly. Several investigators have been pushed on the second to third floor stairway.

Falls Creek Park

Pendleton: Falls Park Dr.

This historic park is home to two residual hauntings. Rachel Harris fell into the creek while being chased by her lover John. She was most likely killed instantly from a blow to the head by the rocks around the falls. John dove in after her only to be pulled down by her lifeless body. The residual haunting of this event is reenacted in the early mornings, usually around 7:15-8:00 am.

In 1824, John Harper and four others were hanged on the north east side for the murder of nine men, women and children. Harper escaped but his friends became the first white men in Indiana hanged for murdering Native Americans. Today, eyewitnesses claim that they hear the men swinging in the wind. EVPs of distressed men crying "No, No!" have also been captured.

Florida (Station)

Anderson: Between CR 375 N at the railroad tracks and CR 200 W (Cross St).

A Native American burial ground sits between CR 375 N at the railroad tracks and CR 200 W (Cross St). Although no official records exist, this area is old and the homes built at this location seem to only have yards (versus buildings) in the area where they burial site would be.

Investigators have taken readings in the area and orbs and shape-shifting shadows have been spotted. Several investigators have reported shadows shifting into wolves, birds and other animals. Residents of the area find arrowheads in their yards.

French Cemetery

Frankton: NE Corner of Washington and Clyde Streets

In 1917 a Madison County woman, May Berry, a Red Cross nurse, was the first American woman to die on foreign soil during the war. She is seen walking through the cemetery and sitting under a number of trees within the cemetery. She is wearing a dress with a white apron over it. Today, the Frankton May Berry Post 469 remains a tribute to her.

Grand Ave

Anderson: At the curve of Grand And Indiana Avenue.

Anderson natives know the curve on Indiana Avenue used to extend across an old iron bridge. At one time it was known as "The Singing Bridge" or "The Humming Bridge" for the noise that tires made as they went across the iron road of the bridge. Many people wrecked cars, motorcycles, and other vehicles on this road. Although the bridge is no longer there, legend states that there used to be a residual haunting of a man who threw himself from the bridge after his fiancee jilted him. Two other incidents are attributed to hauntings. A woman with her children plunged off the bridge in bad weather. Also, four boys ended up falling off the bridge and into the river below. The cries of all these people are heard at various times of the day and night in the area.

Additionally, just a little south west of the bridge was the Brown Street dump. Two twin boys by the last name of Salley were trapped in an old refrigerator there. They are seen playing in the area to this day.

A little further down Grand Avenue, before Broadway Street, is a train trestle. Once a gathering place for picnics, the overgrown area is now host to less savory affairs. A woman was killed when she fell from the trestle and is now said to haunt the area, showing herself as a filmy apparition screaming like a banshee at those she meets.

Grand Avenue and Huffman Court
Anderson: Grand Ave. at curve

These three roads seem to be a hotbed of activity. Huffman Court is next to a backwater swamp just off White River. An empty field had to be crossed before reaching the backwater, which was home to many frog species, a very large golden carp, and several kinds of water birds. If you follow the edge of the backwater you will come to an old abandoned train trestle. Near the trestle are the ruins of a small house and tiny barn. An old woman used to live here with her pony. She used the pony to haul firewood in a small cart and to go to and from a local store. The pony eventually died and was buried in the yard of the house. The old woman put a granite marker. Today you can hear the ghost train clacking down the trestle as well as hear the locomotive's sharp whistle. The old lady is said to be roaming the property sometimes crying and grieving the loss of her pony. Occasionally she will throw pebbles at intruders when she wants to be left alone.

Gruenwald Historic House
Anderson: 626 Main St.

Native America burial grounds are located on this property. Although the official story is that they are under the parking lot to the south of the house, early maps show this to be untrue. The burial ground extends to the house and north of it to the apartment buildings that stand there.

The two story log home (now covered in brick) was built in 1860 by John Berry. The rest of the home was remodeled in the Second Empire style by Moses Cherry in 1873. Martin Gruenwald owned the house shortly after and lived there funtil 1933. The house has had its share of heartache. Gruenwalds' wife, Wilhelmina Christine (Dick) died at 49 of a lung disease. He resided there alone after her death until 1933.

On a full moon there is a lot of ghost activity here. Volunteers feel ghostly presences. Some don't want the living to leave at closing time. The ghosts will position themselves in front of the doors, trapping workers. They believe one of the ghosts is Wilhelmina Gruenwald. She did not want the home changed and now parts of the land have been changed. The electric typewriter seems to have a mind of its own. An attic window is said to be home to an old lady peering out at the mission across the street.

Volunteer tour guides, working alone in the home, have felt they are being followed, and report that it's not unusual to enter the home and find the electric typewriter typing by itself. An internet rumor states that two people must now be on duty in the house because of the hauntings.

Highland High School
Anderson: 2108 E 200 N

A boy is in seen in the old gym (auditorium), usually running or breathless. Sometimes he's seen in the locker room. Legend has it he died of asthma at a sports practice.

Inness Mansion
Alexandria: 601 S Indiana Ave.

The home was built by John Inness, who didn't live to enjoy it. Shortly after the home was finished, he died, and left a pregnant wife, Mary and a daughter named Blanche. When the baby was born, he was named Robert, because the couple had originally wanted to name the child so if it were a boy. As time went by Robert was finally left alone in the home with a caretaker. Robert died in 1977 and the caretaker died in1983.

People have been tapped on the shoulder Cold chills, footsteps, and feelings of uneasiness have been reported. Furniture moves on its own, sometimes coming precariously close to dumping the contents on hapless onlookers. Shadow figures have been seen, including that of a little boy. Hot and cold spots have been detected. EVPs of children and an older man have been recorded.

Lick Creek
Markleville: E 800 S, S500 E and N 975 W

Five white traders killed some Native Americans for their furs to earn an easy buck. Other white settlers found the bodies on their way to church. The men were caught and jailed, except for one, Thomas Harper, who went to Ohio. The other four men were hanged from a tree in the area.

Although it cannot be definitively proven, there is a grove of trees south of E 800 S at this crossroads. It is said the tree from which these men were hung at is in the woods. Investigators report hearing the cracking of necks and seeing bodies swinging from trees.

Markleville (Town)
Markleville: Woods off SR 38 between Lick and Chadwick Creek

In these woods, 10 foot tall man is said to morph into a beautiful woman with black hair and a white gown. She first appeared to two men on January 26, 1896 and has been seen periodically since.

Memorial Circle Wesleyn Church

Anderson: Park and Raible Ave

The church is supposed be haunted- looked like people just picked up and left.

Monroe Street

Anderson: Monroe St. exact location unknown

On Monroe Street, a house that has since been razed was rented by a young woman and her friend. One evening a few friends decided to visit them as well as another tenant in the building. While talking about the Falls in Pendleton and other haunted locations, a copper ashtray scooted across the table. The young woman and her friend said that the spirits were just wanting them to know they were there.

(See Falls Park, Pendleton, Madison Co.)

Moss Island

Anderson: Moss Island Rd. and Anderson Frankton Rd.
(aka Moss Island Mills)

Moss Island Mills used to be directly on the river. For many years because of the mills the Moss Cemetery was called Moss Island Cemetery. The mills provided meal and lumber for the inhabitants. Built in 1836 by Joseph Mullanix, it was preserved long after it was out of use.

Moss Island Mills (razed) is a very dark and foreboding area. The area around Moss Island Road and the Anderson Frankton Rd. is especially interesting. Strange creatures, too large to be native birds, have swooped down on people. Apparitions of men in work clothes and women in prairie skirts are seen on the curve of the road.

Mounds State Park

Anderson: 4306 Mounds Rd.

Dwarfs in blue gowns are seen here. Some people have reported encountering blue-gowned dwarves in the park and nearby along the White River at Noblesville. According to Delaware Indian legend, they are the Puk-wud-ies, a tribe of little people that still inhabit the forest. Many investigators have entered the park only to find that they've entered a time warp and instead of spending a couple of hours investigating, six or more hours have elapsed. Additionally, visitors have been out after dark and have seen various transparent spirits of Native Americans and white men. Two eyewitnesses were hiking in 1975 past the serpent mounds. The birds got quiet and there was a group of native men in the woods close to them. They gestured the couple over and one of them gave the woman an old bead, which she still has today. The men walked off and disappeared.

N CR550 W
Alexandria: N CR550 W

Three girls were killed on this short stretch of road. They had a cat with them. One of the girls died six months after the murders. She would never talk about what happened. Today, the ghosts of the girls are seen in the car on the road.

Nicholson File
Anderson: Broadway Street North of Grand Avenue *(razed)*

Many of the people who used to work in this old plant swear that it was haunted by other employees who died. Various apparitions of dark shadows, transparent partial entities and solid full color ghosts were seen.

Old Anderson High School
Anderson: 1301 Lincoln St.

A young teenager was raped and killed- her screams are still heard. The old part of the school on the second floor has a ghost that will throw things at you. This ghost seems to have moved to the Wig Wam area. At a recent event where Hillary Clinton spoke at the building, several women in the WigWam's restroom reported many rolls of paper towels being thrown, and crashing into the wall.

(See also Anderson High School, Anderson, Madison Co.)

Paramount Theatre
Anderson: 1124 Meridian St.

Originally opened August 20, 1929, this glorious theater is one of the two "atmospheric" theaters remaining in the United States. AS the lights dim, the ceiling is a veritable panorama of twinkling stars and clouds. In full light, visitors are treated to a Moorish courtyard effect. This majestic theater contains one of only three Grand Page Theater Pipe organs left in the United States. Throughout the 1970-80s, this theater deteriorated and after a lengthy restoration, it reopened in 1995.

Today, brilliant art work and decorations aren't the only items gracing the theater. In the dressing rooms, a woman wearing in heavy stage makeup is seen primping, dressed in a corset. A man with a broom walks on the stage and appears in the orchestra pit. The upper balcony is haunted by two mischievous boys who have been caught throwing items into the seats below.

Old Maplewood Cemetery
Anderson: High St. and W. Grand Ave.

The statue of the Hilligoss children bleeds. In the older part of the cemetery, neighbors have seen white shadows moving, drifting from place to place at night.

Old Train Trestle
Frankton: West of Short Street across the river.

In 1947 a young lady was on the bridge contemplating suicide. She had come home to find her husband cheating on her. She went to the train trestle, and waited for a train, then ran out in front of it. On foggy nights you can hear her screaming, and see her walking across the bridge.

Quick City (Town)
Quick City: North of Frankton, on CR 550 W, on the east side of the road.

Once a city for a glass company and its employees, the company was owned by a man named Quick. By giving natural gas away for free, Quick enticed other companies to come to the area. Once the gas boom went bust, so did Quick and all the companies, they left and took the citizens of the area with them.

St. Mary's School and Church
Anderson: 1115 Pearl Street

Built in the late 1800s, the site was used as a meeting center for the Indiana tribes and white men in the early part of Anderson's history.

For years, students, teachers and other staff have seen wispy white and black mists and shadows in the northwest showers and bathrooms. The boiler room has had phantom footsteps since the 1970s and footsteps echo in the hallway. The ghosts are believed to be departed staff and church members.

Sigler Cemetery
Frankton: South side of CR 850N (Cemetery Road), west of CR 575W (Washington Ave.)

The cemetery sits at the end of the road across from some abandoned homes. The Sigler family built the cemetery. Jacob Sigler owned the land where Frankton is now. Frankton was named for Francis "Frank" Sigler who designed and developed it.

Strange orbs fly through the cemetery during the day and evening. Mysterious "strands" of lights are also seen by visitors.

These lights seem to be shimmering strands of ectoplasm in various colors (blue, red and orange have been reported).

State Theatre
Anderson:1303-1316 Meridian St.

Sadly unused, this former theater was built in the 1920s and was home to stage and screen stars. In the 1960s Anderson's downtown went downhill and took this theater with it. For a time in the late 1990s, it operated as a live venue, but seems to have gone belly up with the rest of the town.

From at least the 1960s, the balcony of the movie theater was haunted by a man in a suit. He was known to sit down next to movie goers and scare them by disappearing into thin air. Later, when the balcony was closed due to safety issues, the man moved to the main seating area. After the theater closed, many patrons during the '90s claimed to have seen him in the upper restroom areas. Workers also saw the man backstage.

Swamp Light
Alexandria: CR 400 W and SR28

"The Light" as it was known, came out of the swampy area where this intersection once was. The light started very bright and stayed all night, but returned to the water at dawn. During its time ashore, it would be in the trees, along the ground and in the air. People generally believe it is hunting something. Voices whisper but one can't make out the words. One man was chased home by the light and investigators report the same happening at least a mile away from the place.

Union Building
Anderson: 1106 Meridian Street

Originally built as a department store, it was later refurbished to house offices. In one of the early law offices, a secretary who stayed late on Friday to work on some letters was killed by an irate client, who cut her throat. She was not found until Monday morning by one of the attorneys.

People have seen this woman, dressed in 1940s clothing walking though the offices and spaces that now occupy the building. Additionally, a residual haunting of the act occurs. Many visitors have claimed to have heard her scream and drop to the ground in the early evening.

MARION
COUNTY

Acton Miracle
Acton: Acton and Southport Rds. (NW corner)

On I-74 a man named Bob stopped to put on his rain coat and was struck by lightning. Paramedics were called but no one could revive him. A woman in a black dress appeared with a bible and put it on his chest. He began breathing again, although he was in a coma for many weeks.

The area around Acton used to be part of a spiritualist campground which dated from the 1850s. Now, the Franklin Township Historical Museum owns a dress that may have been worn by the remarkable woman.

Broadripple Park
Broadripple: 1550 Broad Ripple Avenue

Established in 1846, this park is in the heart of the oldest part of Broadripple and was used as an amusement park in which one child was killed in a roller coaster collapse. Today the swings move when no wind is apparent. Phantom Native Americans run through the park and several Victorian women are seen walking through the park.

The Falls at Broadripple
Broadripple: College Avenue

From strife between German and Irish immigrants in its early history to numerous train collisions to fires and murder/ suicides along the Falls, and amusement park accidents Broadripple has had a bloody past.

One of the earliest ghost stories attached to this location is about a Native American who stayed after the majority of his people left. He stayed, as he had gotten along well with the people in the area and he was content to live from the waters and woods around Indianapolis. Apparently he had an enemy or two and he was found with his throat cut along the falls. No one was ever charged in his murder but his figure has been seen in Broadripple at the falls and the park for almost 100 years.

Cumberland Cemetery
Cumberland: Muessing Rd.
Many graves here are from very young people. Investigators have seen orbs and have had mists appear in their photos. Who or what the spirits are is yet unknown although many investigators believe the mists and orbs represent people who are buried in the cemetery.

Action and Atomic Duckpin Bowling
Fountain Square: 1103 Shelby St.
aka Play Action Duckpin

The fourth floor is still home to parties that end when the living enter the room. Footsteps are heard throughout the empty building and the elevator runs up and down the floors carrying unseen passengers. Several patrons have been greeted in the elevator with a cheery "Hello there!" A ghost woman who is attributed to the footsteps also makes occasional appearances.

Holy Trinity Catholic Church
Haughville: 901 N. Holmes St.

Haughville is a gem of forgotten history in Indianapolis. Settled by German, Irish, and later Slovene immigrants, Haughville was named for the Haugh, Ketcham, and Co. Iron works. It has always been an industrial area and a working class neighborhood and it is currently experiencing a slow but progressive rebirth.
Priests indicate visitors "feel people" as if they are happy that they are not forgotten in the history that is Haughville. Some parishioners believe it is the builders of the church.

2910 North Delaware Street
Indianapolis: 2910 North Delaware Street

The Beck family used to have their vases and china thrown around. When the police were called for disturbances they found all in order, then police heard a crash resulting in a shattered mirror. For weeks this type of event occurred. A priest was called to perform an exorcism (most likely a blessing). Now this address is a vacant lot.

Alley
Indianapolis: North of 119 S. Meridian St.

David "Buck" Burkhart killed a man over whiskey at the site in the mid-1800s. The man who was killed is seen gasping for break and a rowdy group of cheers is sometimes heard in the alley. Investigators have captured mists on pictures believed to be the man.

Athletic Club
Indianapolis: 350 N. Meridian St.

Private John Lorenzano who died in 1992 in the building fire, is said to haunt the former Athletic club. Now the building is a set of condos, but at one time, when guests stayed in the building, he would wake people up at night or would be seen walking down the hall. One current resident reports still seeing a firefighter in the building on occasion. During the same fire, an older gentleman died. He is seen walking in the lobby.

Alverna Retreat House
Indianapolis: 8140 Spring Mill Rd.

This structure is a Franciscan retreat. A man with white hair and a dark suit roams the halls. It is believed to be Hugh McKenna Landon in a sailing outfit. Now the area is a private housing development

Athenaeum Foundation
Indianapolis 401 E. Michigan St.

Built from 1896-98, this building was the hub of the German community. Home of the oldest restaurant in Indianapolis, it also houses many spirits. Strange bumps and thumps are heard throughout the building. Staff hear whispers, fined papers missing and have seen tables that have been readied for customers "unset". Grey misty figures roam the second and third floors and shadow people inhabit the theatre. Jolly Werner, a man who died by drinking too much and falling into a fireplace, is seen in the old part of the restaurant. Dr. Helene Knabe, a doctor who spent much time at the location teaching for the North American Gymnasts Union and the Medical College of Indiana has been seen in the east section on the first and second floors. Peter Lieber, of Lieber Beer and the Indianapolis Brewing Company is often seen in the Damenverein Rooms and the Ballroom.

Barton House
Indianapolis: Corner of Michigan and Delaware Streets
aka Delaware Flats

The ghost of Dr. Knabe, a woman who was killed in the building, haunts her apartment. In other parts of the building, lights turn off and on, items move from one place to the other and many people have reported hearing footsteps in their apartments when no one is there.

Benjamin Harrison Home
Indianapolis: 1230 N. Delaware St.

Former home of the president for whom the home is named, the Harrison family bought the lot in 1867 and lived in the home (with exceptions to Harrison's jobs) until 1913 when the children moved to New York. Staff and volunteers report hearing footsteps up and down the stairs as well as seeing a woman in a grey dress wearing a black brooch in the third floor ballroom.

(Note: the home is now a vibrant museum dedicated to President Benjamin Harrison and history.)

Boggstown Cabaret
Indianapolis: 6895 W. Boggstown Rd.

Shadow figures are seen throughout the building. Apparitions of a man and woman appear in the old dressing rooms, lights flicker on and off and visitors report being locked in the bathroom, unable to leave. Visitors hear many strange noises in the downstairs when the crowds go home at night.

Brookside Park
Indianapolis: 3500 Brookside Pkwy S. Dr.

Brookside park was founded in 1903 with a rustic look and feel. The idea was that visitors would find minimal intrusion by the drives that wind their way through the park.

Several spectre figures are witnessed by visitors, including a woman who roams the banks of Pogue's Run. She is seen walking along the bank, a shimmering woman with plain features. On October 19, 1903, Myrtle Wright, a grocery clerk was found dead by Pogue's run. In her possession was a quantity of laudanum, yet none was found in her system. Her cause of death remains a mystery.

Butler University
Indianapolis: 4600 Sunset Ave.
(The university has a great map on its website)

- A ghost named Lydia that hung herself at the Zeta Tau Alpha house (now the Tau Kappa Epsilon house) makes herself known by haunting room #1 and the attic of the home. She moves keys and knocks things off shelves. Electrical difficulties and televisions turning on and off are also part of Lydia's doings.
- A dark, dank tunnel from Atherton Union to Schwitzer Hall used to be a dining hall. The dining hall was closed and the entrances sealed for mysterious reasons. Speculation is that a woman was raped and murdered in the tunnel.
- Jordan Hall is said to be haunted by a frail thin girl with large dark rimmed eyes.

Henry F. Campell Mansion
Indianpolis: 2250 Cold Spring Rd.

A ghostly man is seen in this home.

Cathedral High School
Indianapolis: 5225 E. 56th St.
(aka former site of Ladywood High School)

The current incarnation of Cathedral High School sits on the former Ladywood school for girls run by the Sisters of Providence. Loretto Hall, which used to be the main building of Ladywood reported that lights would turn on and off and a nun would be seen walking the halls and lighting candles in the attic. Today the building is used for classrooms, administration, athletics and storage facilities. Students, faculty and visitors still report mysterious footsteps in the halls and several staff members have reported a glowing light going from room to room after late night events.

Central State Hospital
Indianapolis: Bounded by Tibbs Ave, Warman Ave, Washington St. and Vermont St.
(Central State Insane Asylum; Indianapolis Asylum for the Insane; Central Greens)

Opened in 1848, this hospital started on a bad note and stayed that way (as did most institutions of this sort). From the beginning overcrowding and undertrained/overworked staff made the care of these patients trying. Unscrupulous employees and vendors alike routinely served spoiled meat, dairy and vegetables to inmates. In later years, the institution became outdated and rundown, in addition to lack of training dollars spent on staff and almost every year from its inception, the question was asked "do we close it down". Finally in 1994, after uncovering severe patient abuses and a general feeling that large institutions did more harm than good, Central State closed its doors for good. Since then, the buildings have been vandalized by gangs, misused by ghost hunters and pseudo film makers.

Some of the more famous ghost stories around Central State include a man reporting hand prints on his throat from an attempted choking. A ghost nurse appears in the tunnels. Screams and cries heard at all hours of the day and night and shadow figures move in buildings and power house. People feel dread and sickness on the campus.

Today phantom lights shine near sundown in the windows of the Bolton and Evans building as possibly a sense of things to come in the evening. (Note: These buildings are now gone, but people still experience the feeling of people and investigators capture orbs.) People smell smoke where Seven Steeples burned and people report seeing the reenactment of one inmate stoning another inmate to death.

(Note: The location is slated for renovation and some demolition According to the Indianapolis-Marion County police Department, no one is allowed on site day or night due to too many vandals. No trespassing signs are posted.)

City County Building
Indianapolis: 200 E. Washington St.

In the 1960s a witness was shot in the elevator. Although access to this elevator was curtailed for a time, people reported the elevator as functioning although no power was running to it. The shooting victim has also been seen in the area around the elevator.

Court Street
Indianapolis: Court Street and Pennsylvania Avenue

The figure of H.H. Holmes has been seen in this garage. He was reported to have frequented a seedy hotel that was on the street during his killing years.

(See H. H. Holmes House, Irvington (Indianapolis), Marion County)

Crown Hill Cemetery
Indianapolis: Bounded by Boulevard Place, 38th Street and Michigan Rd. Waiting Station is off Boulevard Place

Similar to Resurrection Mary in Chicago and the dead prom girl asking for a ride, Crown Hill legend tells us about a girl that approaches visitors at the corner of Michigan Rd and 38th Street. She will climb in the back seat and instruct you to her house. When you approach, she disappears. Inside the cemetery a little girl giggles and talks about her horse at the grave of James Whitcomb Riley. Voices of the confederate dead buzz in the area of the Confederate grave site moved from Greenlawn cemetery. The waiting station offers us a glimpse into the paranormal with phantom footsteps, slamming doors, and rustling papers. The filing cabinets that house the immaculate records of the cemetery open and close on their own.

Crown Hill has a lush history that began in 1864 and is the permanent home for President Benjamin Harrison, James Whitcomb Riley, John Dillinger, and lesser known people such as Dr. Helene Knabe (see Barton House entry), a hill that houses over 700 orphans and others. At over 550 acres people come from many different places to enjoy the scenery and reflect.

(Note: This cemetery offers public tours. Due to inaccurate and unauthorized filming, before considering photography or videography for public consumption, not for profit or not, must be cleared through Crown Hill. The cemetery is privately owned and operated and has very strict guidelines of usage of its name, logo and of its interments.)

Davidson and New York Streets
Indianapolis: Davidson and New York Streets

In the few homes in the area many tenants and families report hearing gunshots and the tortured groans of a man. Knowing this area is next to an interstate and not the best of places many scoff and say that it is more human than paranormal. However, at one home in the middle of a winter snow, the tenant heard the shot and the groan and heard a knock at her door with someone saying "Please help me." Grabbing a gun of his own, the tenant walked to the back door and found no one there- no footprints either. The tenant checked the front door and around the house. No footprints but his own were there.

Interestingly, in April 1902, a man named August Hoffman was shot by police at this intersection. On January 5, 1903 Paul Marks, who was a machinist, was found shot through the heart on the railroad tracks that cross New York between Pine St and Dickson St.

Delaware Flats (aka The Barton Center of Hope)
Indianapolis: northeast corner of Delaware and Michigan Streets

Dr. Helene Elise Hermine Knabe was slain in this building on Oct 23-24, 1911. Her spirit has appeared in the kimono which was said to contain her blood splattered by the killer. While the building was under renovation, she moved items that were stored in what was her office. She did not like the clutter. Other people living in the building said she walks up and down stairs and levitates many items throughout the building. An EVP was captured of her saying "It's terrible."

Decatur Central High School
Indianapolis: 5251 Kentucky Ave.

In October of every school year, the school cultivates the smell of burnt rubber and the lights malfunction. The manifestation of a girl is also seen and heard crying in the auditorium. The legend behind these events is a drunk driver that killed a girl named Angie in the vehicle as it drove into the school auditorium in October 1979.

Embassy Suites
Indianapolis: Corner of Washington and Illinois Streets

Once the Hotel Bates was where Abraham Lincoln spent a few evenings, eventually it was made over and rebuilt as the Claypool Hotel, which was one of the very best hotels in Indianapolis. After it was razed, Embassy Suites was built in its place. Throughout the history of these hotels, the makings for ghost stories have been present. Abraham Lincoln's ghost is seen all over the US. In the Claypool two famous murders took place Dorothea Poole was killed in 1954 and stuffed in a dresser and Corporal Naomi Ridings was killed in 1943. Her killer was never caught.

Lights mysteriously turn on and off. A female military officer is seen in a lower level restroom. One woman checked in, went out for dinner and when she came back to her room, found all her belongings repacked on her bed.

English Hotel/English Opera House
Indianapolis: Razed. English Hotel (SW Quadrant of the Circle)/ English Opera House (NW Quadrant of the Circle)

Razed. English Hotel (SW Quadrant of the Circle)/ English Opera House (NW Quadrant of the Circle)

Purported to be one of the best hotels and opera houses in the United States, both were razed in favor of more modern buildings. In the opera house, a former actress practiced her lines and a man fitting Mr. English's description encouraged her. He disappeared before her eyes. In the hotel the ghost of an African American waiter walked the halls. Today, people still report seeing both spirits in these buildings.

Gas Light Inn
Indianapolis: 2280 S. Meridian St.

At one time, this bar was home to a candy store and legend has it that John Dillinger frequented the building during his heyday. Investigators and staff hear phantom footsteps and glass breaking in the basement and in the attic. Visitors have seen apparitions throughout the building including the back room. Once, an earring floated to the bar. One investigator was held in the basement by an entity which would not let her leave. Every time she tried to move toward the door, she was physically pushed back. After a paranormal magician did a few nights of magic in the building staff believed he stirred up something even more terrifying and refused to let him return to complete his engagements.

Green Lawn Cemetery *(now part of Diamond Chain Company)*
Indianapolis: 302 Kentucky Ave.

The cemetery has long since gone but occasionally, a body makes its way to the top of the dirt. Bordered by Kentucky Avenue, White River and West Street, this location has more to offer than fencing. Civil War soldiers were the last to be removed and reinterred at Crown Hill Cemetery in 1933. Because of this deliberate oversight, severl soldiers haunt the employee parking to the back of the building. Inside the building, machinery turns off and on at will and the light dim and flicker with no explanation. Many times, security is called only to find no earthly person has disturbed the building or grounds.

Hannah House
Indianapolis: 3801 Madison Ave.

Alexander Hannah, a former state legislator, built the home in 1858 and bought his bride Elizabeth to the home. Hannah was anti-slavery minded and opened his home to shelter fugitives. Tragedy struck when a lantern tipped over in the basement with the fugitives trapped inside. Instead of opening himself up to the measure of the law, it is suspected Hannah buried the fugitives on his land- or in the basement (although no conclusive proof of either has been found).

Many reports of paranormal happenings have been documented. Strange noises, smells and apparitions are observed here. Alexander Hannah makes an appearance now and then. Once he told a visitor to go back downstairs and mind his own business. Even Elizabeth was seen wearing a dark dress one day and a peach colored dress another time. She is also suspected to be the woman who peeks out an upper floor window. Cold spots move from room to room. The smell of death is attributed to Hannah's stillborn child. Chandeliers, pictures and curtains move by an unseen (and sometimes felt) breeze. Old canning jars stood along the wall in the basement at one time and it sounded as if they were being smashed. When visitors went to look, nothing was amiss. Electrical equipment malfunctions- everything from investigation equipment to CD players. Visitors smell burning wood and see the shadows of fugitives in the basement. People have also been touched in virtually all areas of the house. Other visitors have smelled the cloying scent of roses and lavender.

Hawkeye
Indianapolis: 3200 Cold Spring Rd.
(aka Wheeler-Stokely Mansion; aka Stokely Mansion Conference Center)

A member of the Millionaire's Row, Frank Wheeler (who was part owner in the Wheeler—Schebler Carburetor Company and co-founder of the Indianapolis Motor Speedway) built the home as a summer house. This Arts and Crafts home was completed in 1911. Later William Stokely of the Stokely-Van Camp Packing Company bought the home. Features of the house include a porte-cochere for the automobiles and a Japanese tea garden. Additionally, a roofed walking path for pets remains.
This building has a host of spirits. First, a woman runs out the west doors and into a phantom carriage. On the dog walk to the north of the home, visitors have been pushed to the side by unseen hands. A man walking a dog is often seen on the dog walk. In the foyer, a man without a head is seen. The doorbell rings when no one is there. A light in the library turns on and off for no reason. Frank Wheeler, who killed himself in the master bathroom, is still seen reenacting the tragedy- including the gun shot. Features of the house include a porte-cochere for the automobiles and a Japanese tea garden. Additionally, a roofed walking path for pets remains.

Hedback Community Theater
Indianapolis: 1847 N. Alabama St.
(aka Footlight Musicals)

Once part of Camp Morton, a military camp renowned for mistreating its prisoners, now this theater experiences the ghosts of these mistreated soldiers. Lights turn off and on. Some lights seem to be banging out Morse code. Civil War soldiers for both sides are seen throughout the building, but especially in the basement where a headless soldier delights in scaring people. In the upper part of the theater footsteps are heard, the rattle of swords being unsheathed have been heard and a woman without a head is frequently seen.

House of Blue Lights
Indianapolis: 6828 Fall Creek Rd.

Skiles Test, inventor of the underwater swimming pool light, had a great tragedy in his life. His wife died mysteriously and the legend states he kept her in the house surrounded by blue lights. Many visitors and trespassers stated that they used to see him eating and talking to his wife in the coffin. Test died in 1964 and although people who knew him tried to keep the house as a remembrance, it was razed in 1978. The property is now Test Park. Many people who remember the times state that Test used to hang blue lights all year long because he loved the lights. Other people remember he was eccentric but good man who kept train cars of ketchup. Even more people say that Mr. Test was aware of the rumor and delighted in obliging curious onlookers with his blue lights. Others believe the folklore is untrue. Still, the rumors persist.

People claim to see the blue lights still and the figure of a woman and man walking hand and hand through the area where the house stood. Orbs and mysterious mists are also reported.

Indianapolis Firefighters Museum & Historical Society and Firestation Union Hall Theatre
Indianapolis: 748 Massachusetts Ave.

Located in Fire Station 2 which was in use from 1871 to 1929, the museum provides a great look into firefighter history in Marion County. It is the oldest surviving firestation in Indianapolis and the last survivor of four identical firehouses. Today it hosts fire safety events in addition to historic interpretation. Running footsteps have been heard in and a mysterious fire fighter figure has been seen in the museum area where old equipment is on display.

Indiana Repertory Theatre
Indianapolis: 140 W. Washington St.

The artistic director, Howard, used to jog around the mezzanine. One day he jogged outside in the fog and his nephew is said to have hit him with the car. Today, Howard is heard jogging in the IRT.

Indiana School for the Blind
Indianapolis: 7725 N. College Ave.

As with any institution with a history, the Indiana School for the Blind has had its share of growing and education pains. Suicides, murders in the area and natural death has followed the institution over the years. Many visitors and staff members believe these people are still present. A young, skinny girl is seen walking the grounds. Electrical problems plague the area- lights turn on and off, televisions change channels without reason. Closet doors creak open and closed.

Toilets flush although no one is occupying them.

Indianapolis Public School #18
Indianapolis: 1001 E. Palmer
(aka Abraham Lincoln 18)

Legend states the school is on an Indian burial ground and that the upper floor caved in killing children and a teacher. Visitors report hearing balls bouncing in the school and seeing the class assembled in a line in the gym as if waiting on instructions.

Indianapolis Public School #50
Indianapolis: Miley Ave at W. Market St., next to Indianola Park

Cold spots and mysterious noises are reported inside the school. Outside in the large grassy area, children are heard playing and the squeak of a merry-go-round is heard.

Indiana State Fair Grounds
Indianapolis: 1202 E. 38th St.

In 1862 the state fair began humbly at what is now Military Park. Over time, it moved progressively farther north until it reached its current location by 38th street in 1892. Throughout its life, the State Fair had quite a few tragedies, including a boiler that exploded killing onlookers, race car drivers killed in crashes on the track, murders nearby, and the Halloween disaster of 1963 during an ice show in which a propane tank exploded, killing dozens of employees and spectators.

Visitors and investigators report smelling exhaust near the track. Cold spots are felt and thick mists are reported in the Pepsi Coliseum as well as phantom figures of people from former times walking the halls and sitting in the seats. Lights flicker on and off and now and then the scent of smoke is detected. While attending an event, one visitor had a conversation with a woman in the coliseum. The woman was waiting till the crowd thinned and a woman started talking with her. The visitor talked to the investigator "with great sadness" about the 1963 event. The visitor had a child with her and turned away momentarily to attend her child. When she turned back, the woman was gone. Another ghost of Greyhound, a race horse is heard and seen on the race track as well as in his former stall in the Palin Barn. Elvis Presley is also reported seen on occasion.

Inlow Hall
Indianapolis (IUPUI): 316 N. West St.
(now part of the Inlow Hall on IUPUI's campus)

The West Street and Indiana Avenue area has seen better days. No longer a residential area, it has grown into a concrete monster. Not many remnants of the neighborhoods exist until you reach Ransom Place.

A man has been seen in the building gasping for breath. He is seen in work clothes, unshaven and seems to be backing away from someone. In our research, we found that at 316 N. West St. John Emerson, a lumber dealer, was shot in the right temple by a man who ran away and was never caught. Emerson died February 16, 1910.

James A. Allison Mansion
Indianapolis: 3200 Cold Spring Rd.

Built between 1909-1911 this home was James and Sarah Allison's summer home. James co-founded the Prest-O-Lite company which produced superior car headlights. Additionally he helped design Speedway and a partner in the Indianapolis Motor Speedway. He was also famous for starting the Allison Transmission Company. Now it is part of Marian College's campus.

It is used for a conference center and people can rent it for special occassions. Keys and other objects go missing. Objects move from place to place. And the library is continually rearranged. Legend states that the pool was where James' love child was drowned and a baby's cry is frequently heard here.

Janus Building/Janus Lofts
Indianapolis: 255 McCrea St.

This building has seen much unrest. Situated in the Wholesale District where jobbers filled wholesale orders for stores and other customers, the building was built in 1905 and rehabbed in 2003. Since that time, people have reported strange happenings in these pricy but beautiful lofts. Strange footsteps are heard. In one apartment, lights turn on and water runs. When one tenant asked the entity to stop turning the water and lights on, he was greeted with a chilling laugh as the water and lights turned off and on.

Kessler Blvd and 19th Street
Indianapolis: Kessler Blvd and 19th St.
(seen right and left for 1 block of the intersection)

Eight foot tall beast described as a dog walking on two legs with glowing red eyes. Some witnesses describe the legs of the creature as turned backward; other witnesses describe them as muscular, hairy and turned in at the knee. Best time to see is between 8pm-12am.

LS Ayers Tea Room
Indianapolis: 650 W. Washington St.

Legend has it that a former manager and worker got into a knife fight over a woman and one man was killed. This residual haunting is said to replay itself, even today, despite the tea room being moved to the Indiana State Museum.

Larue Carter Hospital
Indianapolis: Union Dr. on IUPUI Campus (razed)
(Note: The new Larue Cater hospital is in the old VA Hospital on Cold Springs Rd.)

Several employees reported seeing apparitions of early nurses and nuns on the property. The third floor bathrooms had issues as patience and staff frequently heard workmen in the bathrooms but when they would investigate, no one was there.

Lockerbie Glove Factory Lofts
Indianapolis: 430 Park Ave.
(aka Indianapolis Glove Company)

Built in the early 1900s and expanded in the 1920s and 1930s, this buildiing is truly a historic gem. The glove company stayed in business until the recession of 1982 and then moved out of the building. That same year, the building was renovated for home use. People remember the factory and on a warm summer day they remanence that the whir of dozens of sewing machines echoed through the neighborhood. Today, the ghost of one employee haunts the building. She is seen on the elevator and sometimes chats about how the building and business used to be.

Madam Walker Building/Theater
Indianapolis: 617 Indiana Ave.

As the first female African-American millionaire, Madam C.J. Walker ran her beauty product business from this Egyptian and African inspired building. As a theater, the building was once a focal point of the jazz movement on the near west side of Indianapolis.

Although the theater is somewhat mum on what it believes in the paranormal, visitors experience cold spots and see shadow figures in the theater.

Magic Moments Restaurant
Indianapolis: 1 Pennsylvania St.
(Note: No longer in business.)

This former restaurant boasted several paranormal events- tables set for guests that would mysteriously "unset" and cold spots penetrated all areas of the establishment. Legend states that illegal boxing matches were held in which some of the participants died.

231 S. College Ave.
Indianapolis: 231 S. College Ave.

The ghost of one of the former owners of the Milano Inn or possibly a former tenant named Mary plays with visitors in the upstairs room of the restaurant. She touches people on the shoulder, face and she even blows in their ears and their hair! EVPs of various qualities have also been collected.

Mill No. 9 Lofts
Indianapolis: 624 E. Walnut St.

Located in the historic Real Silk factory and later the Printing Harts Center, Inc., there is more than beautiful urban living happening in the buildings. During renovation, the entire mornings work for one construction worker was undone while he was at lunch. Bolts and studs were removed from ceilings and floors. No one connected with the work could be blamed because they were all at lunch together. Footsteps echo through halls and several tenants have reported strange rappings in the wall. One tenant said she played a yes/no game with the rapper and found that it was one of the people who used to work for Real Silk.

Millersville Bridge/ 39th Street Bridge
Indianapolis: 39th Street across from the Indiana State Fairgrounds

Although this bridge is now largely used for foot traffic for the fair, occasionally the sounds of someone splashing into the water and cries of help are heard. In the early 1900s two brothers were fishing. One fell in and as the creek was high and rushing, was carried away. The other brother was never the same. Additionally, the large figure of something described as everything from Bigfoot to a Wampus Cat has been reported under the bridge as well.

Monument Circle
Indianapolis: At the intersection of Meridian and Market Streets

Reports of a small boy are reported. The child has interacted with many people. The ghost of a man who killed himself is said to put people against the glass on the observation deck. Staff report elevator malfunctions and the sound of footsteps on the many stairs when no one is in the area.

Morris Butler House
Indianapolis: 1204 N. Park Ave.

Built in 1864 by John Morris, the area was devoid of other homes until later in the 1870s. The Noble Butler family occupied the house next and resided there in some form until 1957, when the family held an estate auction and left the declining neighborhood. In 1964 the Historic Landmarks Foundation occupied and restored the building over time opening it as a museum.

The sounds of children running though the second floor and a much unused upper turret room is also home to footsteps. Through the magnificent tower of the home, footsteps are heard walking down the tower stairs. One recent visitor reported seeing a hazy figure of a child walk into one of the upstairs rooms and heard the child giggle as if playing a game.

Morton Place
Indianapolis: bordered by 19th and 22nd Streets and Delaware Street and Central Avenue.

This land hosted the State Fair and later became Camp Morton during the Civil War. It was named after Governor Oliver Perry Morton. By 1862 it was a prisoner of war camp which housed over 15,000 soldiers. On the south side of the camp was Camp Burnside which housed the volunteers, invalids and the reserve corps. After the war, the State Fair was brought back to the grounds until 1891. Today it is on the National Register of Historic Places. Many of the homes in this area still date from the late 1800s when it was turned into a neighborhood. Owners report seeing many Confederate and Union soldiers. One woman was in her backyard planting a garden when three Union soldiers in formation walked through her background. She described them as milky white and transparent. Another home owner was surprised to see a Confederate soldier with crutches walk down her main staircase. Yet more people have heard cries of men in pain and heard military calls and cadence during all hours of the day and night.

Murat Shrine Temple
Indianapolis: 510 N. New Jersey St.
(aka Murat Theater; Old National Centre)

Elias Jacoby, a potentate of the Murat died in 1935 and has been haunting the building ever since. He's seen in the Egyptian room in person and as a light emanating from different places in the room. A shadow of a figure in an X position is seen on the Egyptian room stage where a worker fell to his death. People have also reported seeing this figure by the electrical panel of the stage and they report feeling very cold in his presence. Jacoby has also been seen in his box seat in the Egyptian room. and a blue light has moved from his box seat into his painting. Drinks unattended by workmen have been emptied by unseen people. Lights turn on and off by themselves, the elevator runs with no one in it and a portrait of Jacoby changes from young to old depending on the time of year. The portrait has also been seen crying.

Old City Cemetery
Indianapolis: Corner of West and South Streets
aka Greenlawn Cemetery

Now a fence manufacturer, this building is full of unrest. The building itself reports electrical problems although electricians find nothing out of order. Heavy footsteps are heard at all hours of the night throughout the building. Outside in the parking lot, a group of Civil War Soldiers wait for employees to come out and follow them to their cars. Supposedly all the bodies from this cemetery have been reinterred at other places but many people have their doubts.

Old Spaghetti Factory
Indianapolis: 210 S. Meridian St.

Formerly home to several dry good distributors, The Old Spaghetti Factory now hosts more than food! The Banquet room is home to strange noises and light bulbs popping. The locked door in the basement that leads to the city tunnels as well as the women's bathroom is where people hear a baby's cry. Staff and visitors hear kids talking and laughing on a back stairway and in the banquet room. Some people have speculated that these noises come from children who were employed before child labor laws. No proof of this has been found, however it is interesting to note that in addition to dry goods, one of the companies manufactured work shirts and overalls.

Paul Rüster Park

Indianapolis: 11300 E. Prospect St.
(Cemetery next to entrance)
(Paul Ruster Park Cemetery)

Paul Rüster was killed by a train and was buried in the foundation of an old house (near park entrance). Some people have heard him playing a harmonica or have seen him walking on the road and in the park.

Phoenix Theatre

Indianapolis: 749 N. Park Ave.

The theater makes its home in a renovated 1907 church in the historic Chatham Arch neighborhood. Props have been moved, footsteps have been heard and shadowy figures have been seen during rehearsals and performances. Most people believe these spirits are people who have been connected with the church and the theater.

Riverdale

Indianapolis: 3200 Cold Spring Rd.
(aka The Allison Mansion; aka Allison Conference Center)

On the edge of the Marian College campus, the Allison Mansion, built and known as Riverdale in 1909 to 1911, was the summer home to the James A. and Sarah Allison. The home has been used as administrative offices and housing for the college as well as a home for the Sisters of St. Francis. Now, the home is used for special events.

People have reported odd happenings in the building. Items are missing, most notably keys (which a former nun used to collect) furniture and books are rearranged from one place to another. A baby's crying is heard near the indoor pool. Part of the legend is that the Allison's had a baby that drowned in the pool. Depending on the source, sometimes the baby is described as a servant's baby that drowned or was killed because it was either Allison's child or the mother couldn't bear to be a single mother. People have been pushed down the grand stairway and have heard their names called. One of the most compelling pieces of evidence for paranormal activity is the number of people who have held special events in the former home only to have their faces in pictures covered by a mist. The former master bedroom is haunted by Sarah and the billiards room by James. The basement door is known to close and lock when you enter the area. Feelings of dread follow. Candles blow out at events for no reason.

Rivoli Theatre

Indianapolis: 3155 East 10th St.

Built as a Universal Studios theater in 1927, this theater treasure still as some of the original gum woodwork, leaded class and terrazzo. The auditorium accommodated up to 1,500 people which was large for the time. Later the theater was used for live jazz, swing and rock bands.
Many owners state that the building was haunted. Mysterious people would sit in the seats and laugh and talk as if enjoying a show, although none was playing. When asked why they were there, the intruders disappeared. One man walks through a row of seats as though trying to go through a full row only to disappear in a wall. A woman in a white

dress is accompanied by a man in a tux and they sit in the theater as well. The bathrooms seem to have activity as the water turns on and off, toilets flush and conversations with people who are nowhere to be found take place. Cold spots are felt in the projection booth. Lights turn on and off and a light appears in the auditorium that grows dimmer and stronger, eventually to disappear altogether. Other ghost includes "Lady Rivoli" who appears in the projection booth. Electrical problems believed to be caused by the paranormal are also reported. Other noises include muted conversations and glass breaking.

Rock Bottom Brewery
Indianapolis: 10 W. Washington St.

This building was the scene of the Bowen-Merrill fire that killed 13 firefighters in 1890. Today, a burned smell is detected, firefighters from another time have had conversations with customers, staff and bartenders, and cold spots are felt throughout the building.

James Whitcomb Riley House
Indianapolis: 528 Lockerbie St.

James Whitcomb Riley is seen on the stairs and in the sitting room. Sometimes he laughs or smiles at people who witness his apparition.

Old City Prison
Indianapolis: Razed. This jail was the fourth city jail located south of Washington St. at Alabama and Maryland Streets

This old city prison was built in the 1890s and was made of Indiana limestone. One ghost that was widely reported was that of Robert Munson. On August 29, 1906, he was seen by inmates as being thrown against the bars of his cell and later died. But he was the only person in his cell. His death remained a mystery and inmates reported seeing him in the cell. Inmates put into his old cell reported being woken up by Munson reenacting his death as well as being visited by his spectre looking down at them.

St. Joseph's Cemetery/ Calvary Cemetery/Holy Cross Cemetery
Indianapolis: West Troy Ave. and Bluff Rd.

A conglomerate of Catholic cemeteries, this area is home to small children who dart behind tombstones throughout the cemetery and giggle with delight when you can't find them. One investigator visited in winter and heard the children giggling and heard them "step through the crunchy snow". When she looked back, she found small footprints following her. The footprints ended behind a large stone.

St. Joseph's Catholic Church
Indianapolis: College Ave. and Park St.

The legends state that the stigmata occurred simultaneously to 92 witnesses in the church. The church was built in 1871 and left abandoned in the mid 1949 for a more spacious area closer to the congregation.

Footsteps and banging have been heard in this historic building and one group of visitors witnessed the stigmata on the hands of one person after visiting the basement and seeing colored orbs. Another visitor came face to face with the ghost of a priest that walked through him. Curent staff at the restaurant in the building have heard footsteps and seen glasses come off of the bar and drop.

Schoolhouse Square Apartments
Indianapolis: 953 Prospect Street

Originally constructed around 1870 it was started as the St. Joseph Institute and used by the brothers of the Sacred Heart. Many people have heard footsteps throughout the building. One day, several of the tenants heard a measured footstep walk down the hallway and pause at each door. Then the footsteps came back the same way pausing at each door- but this time each tenant heard a knock. When they looked in the hall, no one was there. The brothers seem to still be around as they are seen from time to time walking into various doors and walls.

Sheffield Avenue and Howard Street
Indianapolis: Sheffield Ave and Howard Sts.

The sound of children playing and gunshots are heard at this location around the December holidays. Oddly enough, Claude Baker, who was 12 was shot by Earl Foster, 13, when they were playing holdup- on December 18, 1911.

Spiritualist Psychic Church
Indianapolis: 1415 N. Central Ave.

This former mansion is now a church. The ghosts of many former residents haunt the mansion and several orbs and mists have been captured on film.

Stutz Business Center
Indianapolis: 212 W. 10th St.

Harry Stutz, a player in the Indianapolis automobile industry, built the buildings as part of his factory. Today mysterious thumps and bumps are heard, including footsteps. Cold spots are reported by various tenants and one man reports having seen Harry Stutz himself in a second floor office.

Sylvia Likens House
Indianapolis: 3850 E. New York St.

(Note: Razed in April 2009.)
Sylvia Likens was in the care of Gertrude Baniszewski in the summer of 1965. For three months she endured abuse by Baniszewski, her family and the children of the neighborhood. They burnt her with cigarettes and tattooed "I'm a prostitute and proud of it!" on her stomach. The end came when she was tossed in the basement for days. Trying vainly to scratch herself out of the basement, eventually she passed out. The members of the home threw her into a cold bath and pitched her body on a stinking mattress in the upper front north east side room, where she died of malnutrition and shock from her skin wounds.

Since that time, the home has never kept tenants well and has largely stood empty. In 2003 an organization tried unsuccessfully to form a woman's shelter/education center. From the time Sylvia died, she was seen not only looking out the window but also in the cemetery in which she is buried (see Oak Hill, Boone County entry).

Tuckaway House
Indianapolis: 3128 N. Pennsylvania Ave.

In the Meridian Park neighborhood, this 1906 bungalow was purchased in 1910 by George and Nellie Meier. George was a famous clothing designer and Nellie read the palms of the stars. President Roosevelt, family members and other presidents also had their palms read by her. Nellie even predicted the ultimate demise of Carol Lombard (Clark Gable's wife) before her fateful plane trip from Indiana.

The home has had spirits since the time of Nellie and her spiritualism, but today, guests appear and disappear at will, random screams are heard and a woman dressed in early 1900s clothing appears as well. George Meier and his wife are seen from time to time. Mists and orbs have been captured in pictures as well. One woman staying at the home reported that she dreamed of her room being disheveled by someone and when she woke up, her dream had taken place. Pictures swing and fall from the wall. Additionally visitors have smelled the scent of perfume and roses. Some visitors have picked up EVPs including a woman saying, "it's here" and "not tonight". Other guests have felt a cloying dizziness in different areas of the home. Cold spots are also common.

Union Station
Indianapolis: 123 W. Louisiana St.

This 1880s structure was put on the National Register of Historic Places in 1974. Once a bustling train station, it now houses a few bars, restaurants and is rented in part for events.

A mysterious man believed to be John W Daughterty replays his death on the stairs to the tracks. Security guards are plagued by phantom Civil War soldiers playing hide and seek with them.

In the hotel section in the Pullman cars, people report feeling as if the cars are in motion, heard train whistles and have heard the spirits of conductors asking them to board the train. They have also been jarred awake by unseen hands. Ghosts have been seen entering the train cars, by staff although no one had booked the cars for a stay. Several staff have also heard animal noises coming from different areas of the station and have speculated they could have been stock brought through the station.

Waterbury Neighborhood
Indianapolis: 2901 W. 96th St.

Contains a condominium in which an older woman passed away. Now object are moved, disappear and noises are heard.

West Merrill Street near White River
Indianapolis: West Merrill St. near White River

Visitors report mists and orbs and laughter and singing from men. All sounds stop as visitors approach. In many of the homes across from the area, people see spirits in their home. These spirits have been known to be unhappy and wail. One visitor reports hearing the men, and hearing a woman with them. Shortly after that, a woman's body was found. She had been dead less than an hour.

Wyndam Apartments
Indianapolis: 1040 N. Delaware Street

One apartment has the ghost of an old woman in the kitchen that goes through the motions of making tea. When the woman is present, the smell of freshly brewed tea is also smelled. The apartment bathroom also inspires fear and dread, there a young woman is seen, naked in the bathtub with her wrists slashed.

Zion Evangelical Church of Christ
Indianapolis: 603 N. New Jersey St.

The church and its offices have several visitors. In the bell tower of the church, a women cries as if looking for a lost love. The bell rings when no one is around. Inside the offices, a man paces back and forth at all hours of the night as if trying to memorize a sermon. Doors also slam shut in the offices with no provocation.

1310 North Olney Street
Irvington: 1310 N. Olney St.

Visitors and former tenants report orbs, wispy figures and whispers. Lights would turn off and on at will.

Applegate House
Irvington: 5339 University Ave.

A dark figure of a young boy haunts the house. Sometimes he speaks to visitors.

Benton House
Irvington: 312 S. Downey St.

An old woman sometimes comes out of the house to yell at the children and a woman in a wheelchair is seen and heard on the second floor. One visitor also remembers talking to the woman in the wheelchair who told her about the "noisy children" in the neighborhood.

Bona Thompson Library
Irvington: 5330 University Ave.

Visitors have witnessed Bona Thompson walking through the facility which is now home to the Irvington Historical Society.

Briggs/Johnston House
Irvington: 5631 University Ave.

Owners report footfalls on the stairway and on the upper floor of the home. Some investigators believe a small boy named Joe Johnston (the son of a former owner) and his mother Mrs. Johnston inhabits the home. Visitors have also reported orbs.

Children's Guardian Home
Irvington: 5751 University Ave.

The ghost of a maintenance worker is seen working throughout the building and grounds. A child haunts the building sometimes as a misty shape and other times just as the sound of severe coughing.

John Gruelle House
Irvington: 5738 Oak Ave.
(aka Raggedy Ann House)

John Gruelle was a cartoonist for the Indianapolis Star as well as the creator of Raggedy Ann (based on the works of James Whitcomb Riley. A battery operated doll came to life in this house although it had no batteries. Lights and flashlights turned on for no apparent reason.

Haag's Drug Store
Irvington: Audubon Rd. and Washington St.
(now part of Irvington's commercial district)
(Note: The drug store is no longer a tenant but the district remains.)

Visitors claim spirits of people who passed through the building are still present and guide them to help their businesses.

H.H. Homes Home
Irvington: 5811 Julian Ave.

H. H. Holmes, famous serial killer killed a young boy, Howard Pitezel in the home. A dark presence is reported as well as figures walking through the home. Cupboards open and close at their own whim and voices are heard by the owners. The heat is turned up or off as well.

Thomas Carr Howe House
Irvington: 325 S. Audubon Rd.

Visitors report odd odors.

Irvington Office Center
Irvington: 338 Arlington Ave.
(aka Irvington School #85; aka Loomis School)

Locals know School 85 as the Loomis School, so named for a favored music teacher, George Loomis. He is said to haunt the school slamming doors, opening windows and even tapping doors and walls. Some locals have also seen him from the windows.

Irvington Presbyterian Church/ Johnson House
Irvington: 55 Johnson Ave.

A ghostly choir is seen in the building and the strains of melody heard. The Sylvester Johnson house was part of this same land and razed, yet Johnson seems to continue to visit the church in his ghostly form.

Irvington Theatre
Irvington: 5505 E. Washington St.

In the apartments above the theater, tenants report strange phone calls from people who later were confirmed not at home at the time of the call. Children's voices, crying and the sounds of them playing have also been reported. One investigator was pinched. An EVP of a child's voice was captured. In what was the theater now sits a coffee house. The owner reports chess pieces moving when no one was in the shop and the restroom is haunted by spirits who like to taunt the occupants.

Jesse's Place
Irvington: Building at NE corner of Washington and Ritter Streets
(aka Buffalo Bills)

A man and his pregnant wife were shot and killed here in 1976. Several musicians report feeling an oppressive feeling in the place when they played there after the murders. Additionally one musician who used to carry a gun was punched in the back. He believes it was from the family who died.

Johnson House
Irvington: 263 Audubon Rd.

A music teacher who lived in the home and played the harp is seen from time to time sitting in the turret and her harp music is heard.

Julian Mansion
Irvington: 115 S. Audubon Rd.

Lights are reported as turning off and on, even during the years that the house was left empty after George Julian's death. A man, presumably Julian paces downstairs and workers in hospital garb are seen in upstairs windows. Ghost children have been heard playing.

Julian School #57
Irvington: 5435 E. Washington St.

A ghost named "Agnes" roams the halls in an old dress. People report seeing her during the day and evening as well as hearing her footsteps. Teachers report doors slamming for no reason, hearing music when no one should be playing and lights mysteriously flickering.

Kingsbury Medical Hostel
Irvington: 20 S. Johnson St.

The doctor who treated Madge Oberholtzer lived in this home. When visitors spoke about the doctor, they heard a crash but could find no source for it.

(See Oberholtzer House and D.C. Stephenson Mansion, Irvington (Indianapolis), Marion County)

Lincoln Ghost Train
Irvington: Bonna Ave. parallels the tracks.

(Note: As of April 2009, much of the tracks have been taken away in favor or paved trails. In Irvington town, the track is still present.)

In April of each year, visitors and residents claim to see the Lincoln Funeral train that passed through the area in 1865. Some witnesses report seeing full color and black and white apparitions on the train; other witnesses report skeletal figures. A small boy is also seen from time to time waving from the train. Some investigators theorize this was a boy who tried to cross the tracks in front of the train and died for his effort. A man who killed himself at the same location is seen by visitors as well.

Masonic Lodge #666
Irvington: 5515 E. Washington St.

Construction workers reported dark shadow figures walking in front of bright lights. Other workers felt someone touch their hands, arms or even tap their shoulders. Doors open and close on their own, sometimes accompanied by shadow figures walking through them. A film production company reported a brand new refrigerator not working and called in a repairman to fix it. Determining it was not working but had no mechanical reason it shouldn't work, it was determined to move the film stored in it to a different place, they did so. When they returned to the refrigerator it was working properly and at the proper temperature.

Oberholtzer House
Irvington: 5802 E. University Ave.

Home to Madge Oberholtzer, who was killed by D.C. Stevenson. She is seen in her home and throughout the town of Irvington. She is especially seen on stormy nights in the upstairs windows in the room she was laid out in after her death. Occasionally, when Madge is seen on the streets, she will speak with passerbys.

(See D.C. Stevenson entry, Irvington (Indianapolis), Marion Co.)

Roof House
Irvington: 5980 University Ave.

Visitors report seeing a ghost kitten. Former owners report doors and windows opening and closing with no reason. A translucent woman is seen near the attic.

Southeastern Irvington
Irvington: Bounded by Ritter St., Brookville Rd., Arlington Ave. and Beachwood Ave.

The sound of horses are heard, presumably looking for John Brown, a farmer who was killed by John Wade and Brown's wife "Bloody" Mary Brown. The motive was John's love and Mary was implicated with him in the trial. Both served life prison sentences.

South Irvington Circle
Irvington: Audubon Rd and University Ave.

Visitors have seen a milk white figure of a woman. Visitors also hear a phantom gunshot, presumably attached to a man that killed himself at the circle. A mysterious old man dressed in late 1800s clothing and sporting a beard walks through the area. Additionally, there was a fire at a school that sat on the site and although there is no official record of any deaths, visitors have reported ghostly boys playing leapfrog and some people report having had their hats removed by unseen hands.

D.C. Stevenson Mansion
Irvington: 5432 University Ave.

Former home to D.C. Stevenson, an active Klansman who thought he was above the law. He was convicted of the rape and death of Madge Oberholtzer, a state employee. During her kidnap and abuse, Stevenson kept her in the carriage house of his home. In 1986 two men were found dead in the same carriage house. Today lights turn on and off in the carriage house. Visitors report the sounds of merriment and shadows are seen in the main house. Investigators report smoke rings and the smell of cigar smoke throughout the home. (Stevenson loved cigars.)

Old Firestation
Oaklandon: NW corner of Oaklandon Rd and Broadway St

At last count, this was now a church youth center. The old firehouse has been remodeled over time. The doors in the building frequently open and close. The bay doors open and close without anyone around. In the old part of the station, it is often very cold. Lights turn off and on. Bangs, knocks and other noises happen often.

Nicholson- Rand House
Southport: 5010 W. Southport Rd.

This home has several legends. The owner's daughter was killed by a car and decapitated. The girl was shot by hunters. The girl fell from the second story balcony. In any event, the story continues that the family sold it and the family who bought it cut it in half and moved it. When it was being moved, a photographer captured a photo that appears to have a little girl in the upper window. It's been widely reported that other people have captured this same image and that if you go into the room, it is very cold and breezy in the room, even with the window closed. When the house was moved, many people felt the presence of the girl and the spirits from the cemetery behind the house. Some investigators reported odd EMF readings in the house while the power was disconnect (although no mention of other sources outside of the house were investigated).

Train Tracks
Southport: Between Southport Rd and Stop 11 Rd.

A woman's baby was killed by a train when it toddled across the tracks. In grief, she threw herself in front of another oncoming train. You can hear her screams and see her run to her death.

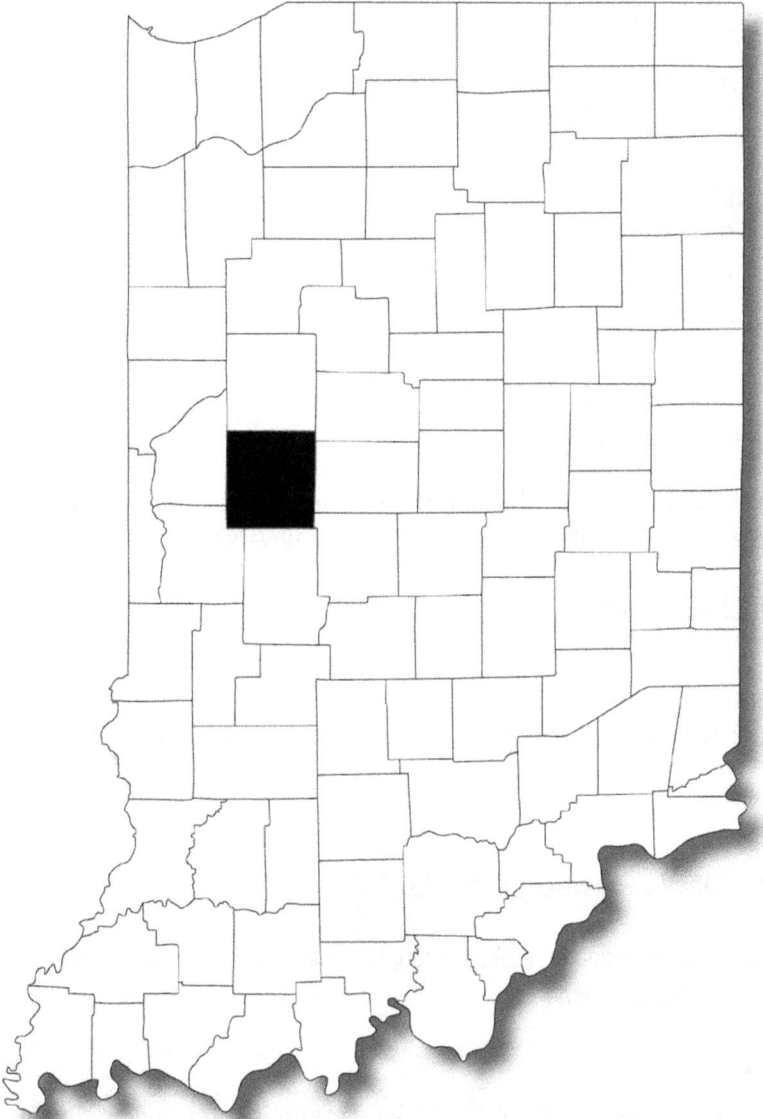

MONTGOMERY COUNTY

Ben Hur Nursing Home
Crawfordsville: 1375 S. Grant Ave.

Residents and staff talk about two children who speak to and annoy them. A nurse who used to work there also is seen moving through corridors and checking on patients.

Culver Union Hospital
Crawfordsville: Near 306 Binford St.
(aka St. Claire Medical Center)

Signs of haunting in the morgue area of the hospital.

Davis Bridge
Hibernia: Davis Bridge Rd. near S600W

The land near this home used to host many rodeos. The original house burned down and the ranch home was built in its place. Legend says that people in the area die in threes. Lots of negative energy is felt here.

Lester B. Sommer Elementary
Crawfordsville: 3794 W. US 136

A girl lived on the property before Sommer's School was built. She was tortured and abused by her father and tried to run away. Her father shot her and buried under the house on the property. Today, lights flicker in a restroom and you can see her shoes under the stall door.

Michael Cemetery
Crawfordsville: On W. Offield Rd west of CR S325 W

Investigators capture mists. One investigator walked through a visible mist and felt hands on her face; however, the photographs did not capture the mist.

New Market Trestle
New Market: East of US 231 and south of S 400 W. Trestle is over Offield Creek

A phantom train whistle and the sound of brakes are heard. Several blue figures skirt the water. Some people believe these are the people who died at the trestle. Others believe they are elemental.

Oak Hill Cemetery
Crawfordsville: 392 W Oak Hill Rd

Investigators report orbs throughout the cemetery.

Offield Monument
Balhinch: Offield Monument Rd. Near Spooky Hallow Bridge.

The date on the monument changes on Halloween.

Old Jail
Crawfordsville: 225 N. Washington St.

Doors are heard opening and closing. Conversations with unseen people occur. An "evil" chuckle is heard in the lower level of the building.

Silver Dollar Bar (and Apartments)
Crawfordsville: 127 S Washington St (no buildings in lot now) Corner of Washington and Pike

In May 2007, a devastating fire destroyed the entire 100 block of South Washington Street- including the historic Tommy's Bar (as it was known to Wabash College folks). It was known more recently as the Silver Dollar Bar. Thirteen apartments were destroyed and one person died in the fire. The town was devastated, as the bar was known for its "come as you are" attitude.(Leslie) Eric Largent, a resident of the building, died in the fire trying to save others in the building. The firefighters that battled the blaze had to leave his body in the building as it was too unsafe to retrieve it. They used thermal imaging to detect people and survivors. People in the neighboring businesses have seen him walking through their stores. Additionally, other people have seen him leaning against the neighboring building looking out over the empty lot. When approached, he looks very sadly at the people and disappears.

South West Corner of E. Main and S. Green Streets
Crawfordsville: Building at SW corner of E. Main and S. Green

Originally this building was a bank. A child's ghost haunted this building when it was a restaurant. An electrician would not go in the basement because of the "spooky ghost".

Spooky Hallow Bridge

Balhinch: Offield Monument Rd.

(aka Spooky Hollow)

Several legends exist about this bridge. This bridge is home to the boyfriend who scares his girlfriend by making up a scary story and saying the car died. He gets out of the car and the girl hears a scraping noise. When she leaves the vehicle she sees him hanging from a tree and his hand is scraping the roof of the car. If you go to this location, your car will die.

At one time, this bridge was a covered bridge (a new one was built later). Depending on the story, either a black man or a white woman was hung from it. If you flash your lights three times, you can see the hanging person.

Investigators capture unexplained mists.

Wabash College

Crawfordsville: 301 W Wabash Ave

Investigators have witnessed a young man with an arm that seems to be out of its socket and dangling lower than the other. His clothes are tattered a bit and he seems to acknowledge the investigators but does not talk to them. Obs are also seen.

MORGAN COUNTY

Brick House
Mooresville: 8 E. Washington St.

Visitors have reported hearing footsteps in this old building. Doors slam and windows close on their own.

Draper Cabin
Martinsville: Morgan-Monroe State Forest (6220 Forest Rd.)

Folklore includes a murder that occurred years ago. Another story includes a murderer that has been stalking the cabin for 130 years, waiting for victims. Although these stories have yet to be proven, investigators and visitors have reported seeing transparent wolves around the cabin and a shimmering pink woman walking through the woods at night. The best times to visit this cabin are in early spring and fall when the pink lady makes her most copious appearances.

Gravity Hill
Mooresville: Keller Road off the US70 Monrovia exit

A woman and her son were killed on the road while changing a flat tire. The ghosts of both greet people at the bottom of the hill. People claim if you put your car in neutral at the bottom of the hill, something will pull you to the top. Variations of this include naming the woman as a Native American and her grandson. The child was playing in the road and as the grandmother tried to get to him, they were both killed. People have reported EVPs of a woman screaming, a little boy singing and cries of help.

John Dillinger's old family home
Mooresville: The town of Mooresville has grown around the area and the home has long since been razed.

A ghost group is seen picnicking under a tree. Laughter and shouts of happiness are also heard. On May 22, 1934 John Dillinger visited his family for a picnic before his fateful trip to Chicago which ended his life.

Stepp Cemetery
Martinsville: Morgan-Monroe State Forest (6220 Forest Rd.)

The wife of a local doctor died in a crash on Liberty Loop Rd (aka Mahalasville Rd., aka Cramertown Loop) road in 1936. Her infant died and was buried in Step Cemetery. The woman went insane and spent her time at the cemetery at her infant's grave. Sometimes called the "Black Lady" she is seen shrouded in black, sitting on the stump and rocking her infant. Other times the story is said to be a woman grieving over her husband or daughter. Many people have visited and investigated the cemetery. Some in search of the Black Lady but some in search of Bigfoot. People have reported mists that stall cars and drain electronic batteries. The Black woman is said to chase people, cry and scream. Other versions include a murdered road worker or teenager.

Visitors also experience bad feelings, nausea and vomiting. Temperature changes, strange breezes and a sense of darkness in the sun is also reported. Orbs, apparitions of the woman and streaks of light have been captured on film. EVPs of crying have also been recorded.

PARKE COUNTY

Beacon Hill Cemetery
Rockville: US 41 and CR 50 W
(aka Crying Baby Cemetery)

Cries of a mother are heard. Sometimes you can hear a baby cry.

Bellmore Schoolhouse ruins
Bellmore: The only thing left of the school is the sidewalks, out houses and a part of the sign that tells the date of the school. There is now a mobile home on the property.

Changes in temperature (from hot to cold) are experienced. Investigators have captured a boys screams. It is believed he was killed in the boiler room. Bricks and dirt fly at visitors.

Billie Creek Village
Rockville: SR36 west to Rockville

This location is a museum and contains several buildings that predating the Civil War all the way up to the early 1900s. The village is full of everything from translucent apparitions seen at night to the odd solid apparitions seen with tour guests. One guest reported staying in the schoolhouse after the other guests left the building. She was looking out one of the windows and saw an apparition of a man behind her. It startled her as she thought she was alone. When she turned, he was gone. The woman turned back to the window to see him behind her again. She heard the man clear his throat, and as she turned to say something to him, she saw quickly him and then his form disappeared.

EVPs of children playing and a woman talking about needing more flowers have been captured by investigators.

Bridgeton Bridge
Bridgeton: Near CR 780 S

This 245 foot red double-spanned bridge witnessed a horse throwing a buggy and its female rider into one of the arches, killing her. Additionally, bootlegger Willie Aikens was hung from the structure. Orbs signifying spirit activity have been captured. EVPs of a moaning man have been heard. The frightened cries of a woman and her spooked horse have also been recorded.

Diamond
(See Brazil, Clay County)

Mansfield (town)
Mansfield: On SR 59 between CR 43 and CR 324

People walk through this town as ghosts from a different time. Wagons and horses are heard. Visitors hear murmurs of conversation. Rocky Fork is known for its green light bridge ghost.

Mecca Tavern/Mecca Bridge

Mecca: 4854 W Wabash St (CR 275 S)

Visitors see and photograph orbs at this site where bootlegger Willie Aikens died (he was hanged from the bridge.)

Missing Death Tracks/ Harrison's Rosedale Tavern

Rosedale tracks: West and Middle Streets. The old tracks have been removed but ran just west of West St. across Middle St.

Tavern : 113 Middle St

(aka Rosedale Tracks)

In the 1960s a woman was hit by a train while walking by the freight tracks. She was found later by her husband. The woman comes back to replay her death, and also frequents the nearby tavern she and her husband owned. Sometimes she talks to drunks and then disappears.

Sim Smith Bridge

Montezuma: On CR 44/ W40 N, south of US36

Built in 1886, this bridge is home to a Native American girl was run down by a horse on the bridge. She appears as a residual haunting replaying her death about halfway through. This bridge, which spans Leatherwood Creek, and was once a main road between Rockville and Montezuma, also hosts a Native American spirit with a papoose. Reports indicate this ghost will walk with visitors or will disappear as it approaches people. EVPs of horse's hoofs, jangling bridles and a man have been caught. Many unexplained photos have been taken.

Turkey Run State Park

Marshall: Turkey Run State Park on Sugar Creek (off SR 47)

Turkey Run is named for the wild turkeys that used to congregate in the canyons (called "runs"). In the early 1900s, Johnny Green, an old Native American, used to go to people's homes and tell tales of old Native American conflicts with the settlers. One day, he went to Goose Rock at the mouth of Turkey Run. Mr. Pruett, a disgruntled husband of a woman he had told stories to, shot him. He fell and was trapped under the rock—his spirit is said to roam the shoreline.

PUTNAM COUNTY

Boone-Hutcheson Cemetery
Greencastle: North of CR600S east of S CR375W
(aka Boone Hutch Cemetery)

A police officer from the 1950s carries a blue light through the graveyard. A nearby cave that runs under the cemetery has a ghostly figure protecting it.

Known to locals as Sellers Cave and University Cave, legend has it that the cave at the cemetery runs to DePaw University. A house on campus allegedly has a sealed up tunnel to the cave. Some people believe this legend is confused with the University's involvement in the Underground Railroad. Still, some people believe that John Dillinger used the cave as an escape route and hiding place.

Brick Chapel
Greencastle: 5 miles north of Greencastle on US231

One of the best-kept ghostly secrets is a piece of property behind Brick Chapel north of Greencastle. An old brick house stood there until recently. This site received national attention in 2000 on an ABC special, "World's Scariest Ghosts."

Two well-known paranormal investigators named Guy Winters and Terry Lambert worked for ABC Television. They shot still photographs and videotaped footage of the old brick home. Several photos showed a woman in pink glowing in an upstairs window of an empty room.

However, there are some who claim to have parked along the side of the field and seen pink balls of light dance across the field. The driveway is currently gated and locked. No Trespassing signs are posted.

Cloverdale Cemetery
Cloverdale: South side of SR42 at CR175E

A couple of women were driving at midnight through the cemetery and saw a man bent over a casket under a tarp. He turned to look at them and they got scared. When went back for a second look, the man had disappeared.

Seven sisters are buried here. If you go around their graves seven times your wish will be granted. Several people have broken pieces of the headstones; when they try to put them close to the bigger stone, it is like a magnetic opposite polar effect is occurring. Temperature changes and strange cold spots are also reported. A hooded black figure appears out of nowhere.

Some investigators have reported taking "something" back with them. The begin having issues at their own homes, including seeing shadow figures and smelling rotting flesh.

DePauw University

Greencastle: DePauw University has a great map of its campus on the university website.

This university was founded in 1837. At least three janitors from different decades have quit because of the hauntings.

In the library, Governor Whitcomb watched over his rare book collection until it was placed in a restricted area.

The library is haunted by a very possessive spirit. In the early 1900s, a student at the old library took a book called The Poems of Olson. A ghost appeared to the student demanding its return. And so it was. This has been reported by many students over the years.

Dick Huffman Bridge

Reelsville: West of US231 on US40, turn south on CR450W. The bridge is east of 600W
(aka Wetky Bridge)

This bridge was built in 1880 and is 265 feet long. Originally it was known as the Wetky Bridge because a mill of the same name was nearby. An old man haunts the bridge. He got drunk one night and fell off the bridge thinking he could fly or walk on water.

Edna Collings

Clinton Falls: Outside Clinton Falls
(aka Edna Collins Bridge)

This 80 ft. bridge was built in 1922 by Charles Collings after the original concrete bridge washed away. Edna Collings liked to swim in the water and jump off the old bridge. Her parents would pick her up when it was time for her to leave. One day the girl drowned. When her parents came to pick her up, they were devastated. Another version of the story says she was raped and killed. If you honk your car horn three times, she will get in the car with you. She is also heard splashing and laughing. Cars have been pushed and door locks flip up and down uncontrolled. The girl has also been seen looking at you from outside the car.

Fern Cliff Nature Preserve

Reelsville: Unknown
(aka Reners Quarry)

An explosion the mine killed over 40 people. The sounds of the explosion and dying men are still heard. This area is near the cliffs in the nature preserve.

Forest Hill Cemetery

Greencastle: Cemetery Rd. to Forrest Hill Cemetery

Pearl Bryan haunts the cemetery. She was killed in 1896 by Scott Jackson and Alonzo Walling after a failed abortion attempt. Pearl told her friend William Woods that she was pregnant by a mutual friend, Scott Jackson. When Jackson found out, Pearl was subjected to a chemical abortion (substance unknown) and an abortion by dental tools. When it was clear she was going to die, Jackson and Walling killed her, then dumped her body in Fort Thomas Kentucky. Her head was never found. She is buried in Forest Hill Cemetery. It is said she walks around the cemetery trying to find her head.

Four Arches
Greencastle: Located west of Greencastle not far from Fern Cliff

The body of a murdered woman buried in the cement when it was built of the train trestle/tunnel. Her figure is seen walking through the tunnel. At other times a phantom train runs through the tunnel. Reports have been made of hearing the whistle echo and feeling the wind blow through the tunnel, although sometimes it is not seen.

Locust Hill
Greencastle: Six miles north of Greencastle on US231
(Note: This building is a private home.)

James O'Hair (O'Hara) built the home and it was in his family for 153 years. Notable guests include William H. Harrison, Miami Chief Cornstalk, and Squire Boone (Daniel's brother). Today it is an antique shop. The ghost of the man an O'Hair daughter fell in love with inhabits the house, along with other spirits. Rocking chairs and candles have levitated and been thrown by unseen hands. A Confederate soldier is often seen as have two women in long white dresses.

RANDOLPH COUNTY

Greenville Pike
Bartonia: On Greenville Pike: At the stop sign turn right at the first gravel road turn left

A headless horseman rides over the bridge. He is said to carry his head in his hand. As he passes by, he laughs maniacally. He's also reported as very good looking. Before his appearance, several women report feeling someone kiss their hands. He also chases you over the bridge and disappears.

Mobile Home
Randolph County: 1475 S. Randolph County Road 750W

A woman named Angela was either murdered or shot herself in the head inside her mobile home. Her ghost is said to roam the area. An EVP was heard asking where Veronica was. (This is one of Angela's daughters.)

Ridgeville Road
Ridgeville: Ridgeville Rd.

A house in the woods is rumored to have blood on the walls. Legend states that several murders happened in the house. The nearby cemetery has a bridge and a creek that runs through it. The man who murdered his family drowned them in the creek. The woman is supposed to appear as an apparition or her wedding ring falls onto the bridge.

Sleepy Hollow Road
Ridgeville: This location is tucked away in between fields. Between W800N and W700N (the north and south boundaries) and N400 W and N300W (the east and west boundaries). There is a small lane on the W700N side that takes you back to a grove of trees, on the NW side of those trees is another path that takes you to a larger grove of trees. Both areas are considered Sleepy Hollow.

People have reported being chased by zombie-like creatures, suspected to have been a part of a non-descript accident in the early 1970s.

RUSH COUNTY

State Road 44 Slaughter
Rushville: SR 44 three miles east of Rushville

On November 15, 1941, a Greyhound bus crashed head-on with an automobile. Nine people were killed in the fiery crash. Investigators have recorded orbs and orange mists in the areas, especially around the anniversary of the crash.

Three Mile and Carthage Roads
Carthage: Three Mile and Carthage Roads

A farm hand for the Stevens family who owned the land was robbed of his weekly wages and killed at the intersection of Three Mile Road. Locals began to see his ghost at the intersection counting his money.

Some believe this is not the true story, but rather a rug salesman, Sam Abood, was robbed for $700 (but not killed) at the same location.

People who have investigated the location have reported a mist and have captured orbs on film. No one has spoken to the farm hand or the salesmen...yet.

SHELBY COUNTY

Boggstown Cabaret
Boggstown: 6895 W Boggstown Rd.

This cabaret is full of family entertainment. The building itself is from 1873 and a Red Man's Lodge. Next door was the Seventh Day Adventist Home for Unwed Mothers. It was also a general store and barber shop.

Investigators have captured orbs, and video of shifting shadows. One family who took pictures at the cabaret found a strange mist in a photo. It appeared in a shape of a short person standing next to their daughter.

E River Rd.
Waldron: E. River Rd., SW of Waldron

A transparent male apparition walks along the road asking for help.

Electric Bridge
Rays Crossing: Off of E. Union Rd. on E. Short Blue Rd.

People report seeing a man on the bridge. He disappears when approached.

Kopper Kettle Inn
Morristown: 135 E. Main St.

Known for chicken dinners, this former tavern and hotel was once a stop on the Underground Railroad (the tunnel leads to the house next door). The building was originally the Old Davis Tavern, then the Valley House, and in 1923 given its current name. The Big Brother, Yellow New, and Music Rooms have reported paranormal activity. Women in Victorian and prairie style clothing have been seen. In the Big Brother room voices as if from a party have been heard, and in the Yellow New room, an indelicate burp was recorded.

Lady Victoria Hamilton House
Shelbyville: 132 W. Washington St.

A little girl haunts the entire building, which used to be Italians Gardens. She was in a black dress and liked to knock pots and pans off tables and open drawers, throwing utensils around. Now and then she likes to scare you by screaming as if she's throwing a temper tantrum. For a time, the third floor was a living area with an old rocking horse that would move on its own.

Private home
Waldron: Unknown location

The home was built in the 1920s. Mysterious figures are seen darting around the home. Children are found playing in dining room. Three people from original family died and had funerals in the home. Two children who lived in the home had nightmares in which one of the apparitions that had been seen by his parents entered his dream. Footsteps are heard upstairs when no one is there. Feelings of dread precipitate the paranormal events.

Tanglewood
Shelbyville: Unknown location

Paul Tindall used to play an organ in his home. After his death, people swore he was still at home playing the organ and the lights in the home would come on at odd times.

Twins House
Shelbyville: Unknown

The location of this house is unknown. Some people believe it is the Federal style house on Polk across from the courthouse. Other people believe it is the house on the north east corner of Franklin and Miller Streets.

Many theories A father killed his wife. Twin boys killed their dad. On July 4, 1940 the boys stabbed each other. Supposedly on July 4 you can see the reinactment of this. Throughout the year the boys are seen at the windows of the house.

Union Road (Haunted House)
Shelbyville: IN44 NE to Rays Crossing. Turn left at N 600E to CR250N and turn left. Follow road around curve (Now N 575 E) to E. Union Rd. Turn right. You'll go over 2 bridges. About 5 miles down E Union Rd, a boarded up white house with barbed wire stands.
(aka the KKK House)

Several legends are associated with this house. One story is that a little girl was accidently shot in the house. The second story centers around two teenage boys that went insane after their father killed their mother. On July 4, 1940 the boys who stabbed each other to death. Other history about this home centers on KKK activity. A Klansman lived in the house with his daughter. She was dating an African-American. The father caught them and he killed both of them. Still another story says the girl killed herself after her father killed her boyfriend. The bloodstains are supposed to be in the upstairs bedroom. Other legends include KKK members killing people in the house and in the basement. The basement is supposed to have nooses in it.

If you stand next to the house, you can hear scratching from inside as if something was digging its way out. Murmurs are also heard inside the house. You can also hear two young men screaming in pain. Mists are seen in the house, and gunshots are heard.

Waldron Junior-Senior High School
Waldron: 102 N East St.
(aka Waldron Middle School)

Three boys were playing in the school and they locked one inside a closet with chemicals. The boy drank the chemicals, thinking they were water. By the time the boys remembered to get him out, he was dead. Now he walks around the gym. Sometimes he is seen in the closet.

Werewolf Hollow

Rays Crossing: IN44 NE to Rays Crossing. Turn left at N 600E to CR250N and turn left. Follow road around curve (Now N 575 E) to E. Union Rd. Turn right. Turn left on N575 E again. At 400 N turn right (turns into Short Blue Rd. Drive to bridge.

Growls are heard from 7-10 foot tall beasts with grey, white or black hair. A ghost of a man will scratch your car if you get too close to him as you pass by. He will sometimes warn you not to go back down the lane. Orbs are present. Orange and yellow mists occur. Another story says a boy went to the mailbox near the hollow and he was hit by a semi while crossing the street. Today he still crosses the road looking for the mail. Finally, a couple pulled off the road near the creek. They heard scratching on the car door. The man got out to see what was going on. Suddenly the woman heard screaming. She drove away and her boyfriend was never found.

White House
Shelbyville: Off 250 North on Union Rd.

A girl killed herself in the house. A permanent blood stain seeped into the floor. People hear scratching, footsteps and eerie laughing.

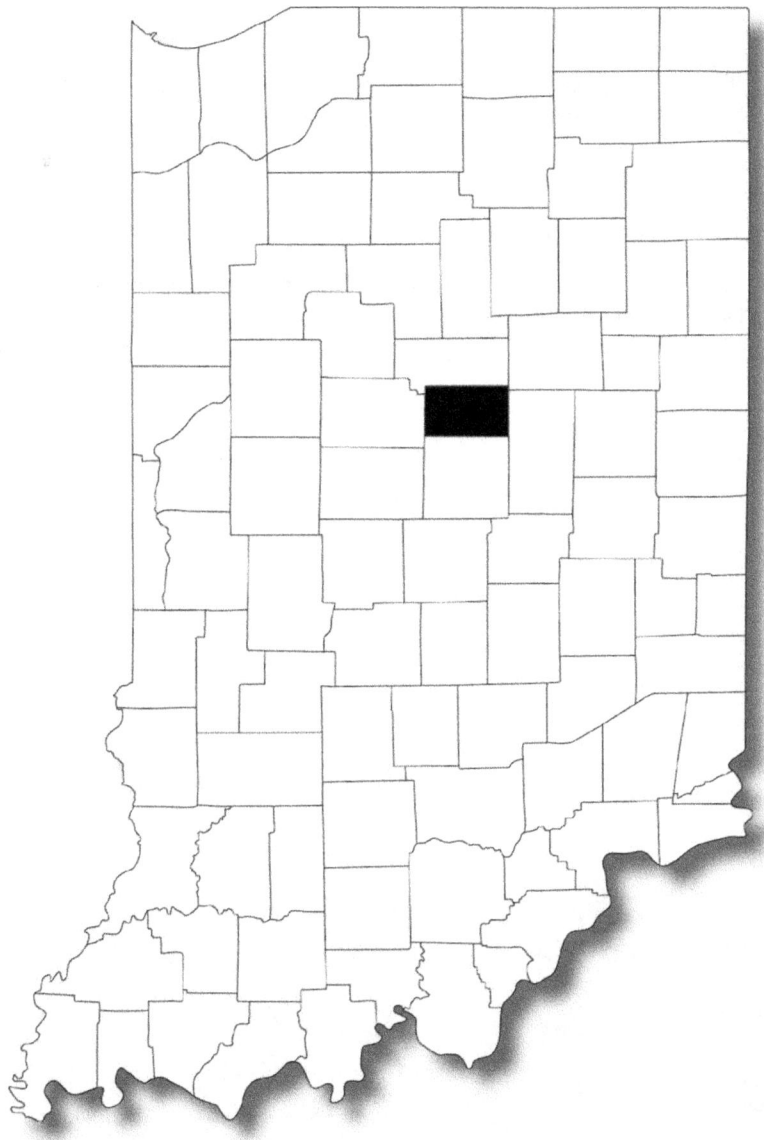

TIPTON COUNTY

Old Factory
Sharpsville: E. Elm St by old train tracks

There are reports of women looking out the abandoned factory windows. The banging of metal on metal can be heard. People can be heard talking when no one is around.

Tipton Courthouse
Tipton Town Square

Security and visitors report a man who was imprisoned in the basement dragging his leg and walking up the stairs. One woman was rudely slapped in the face before a wind blew past her.

UNION COUNTY

Hanna House
Dunlapsville: 3130 S. Old Dunlapsville Rd.

Not to be confused with Hannah House (see entry in Marion County), this early 1800s home was built by Captain John Hanna. A woman named Jenny haunts an upper bedroom. She is seen in a long white dress. She appears in many pictures taken by visitors in the form of mists and orbs.

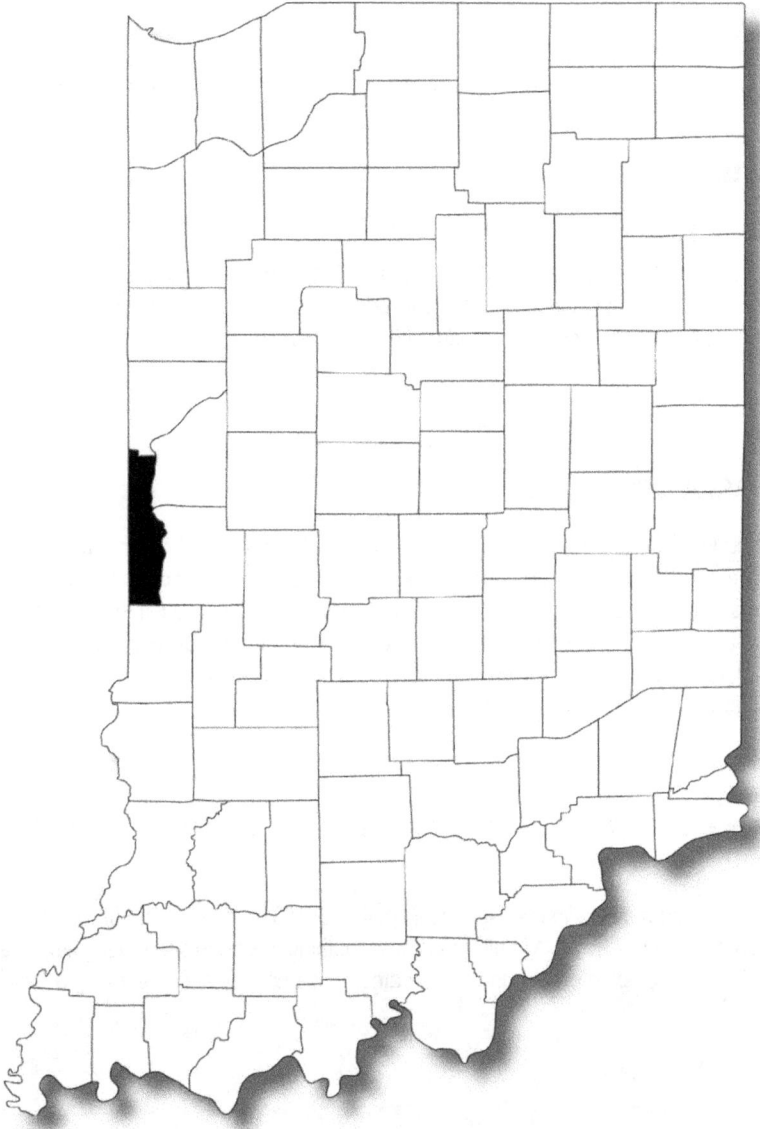

VERMILLION
COUNTY

Ernie Pyle State Historic Site
Dana: 120 Briarwood St.

The tracks by grain elevator are home to a transparent man. He will spit at you and yell if you follow him.

Helt's Prairie Cemetery
Newport: One mile west of IN63 on 1050 S. Rd. (south side of road)

This cemetery was started about 1817. It was donated by the family of Rev. William James. Notable burials are Antoinette Stover (Grandmother of Pres. Dwight D. Eisenhower), and the only person ever executed in the county. During the day, small children dart between the headstones and at night, an older, stooped gentleman is seen walking through the cemetery.

Lake
Cayuga: IN63 and E. Maple St. in the curve

The area around the lake is haunted by several children who are seen walking. Legend has it that the children died of illness in the mid 1800s. Their parents were overcome with grief and could not be consoled. Several mothers killed themselves here. Investigators believe the children are stuck between this world and another, are looking for their parents. When the children manifest, the temperature drops between 10-20 degrees even on warm days/evenings. EVPs of children talking about school and chores have been captured. One EVP captures a child asking, "Where are they? Where is mama?" another child answers "They're gone. They left us."

Thomas Cemetery
Newport: 2 miles north and west of Newport, Indiana on SR 71 and Hopkins Rd.
(aka Newport Cemetery)

Named for Philemon and Catherine Thomas, the first burial was Eli Thomas in 1831, the father of Philemon. The cemetery has six additions in all, and covers almost 17 acres. A family in Victorian clothing has been seen sitting next to a gravesite in the first addition (south side). They do not interact with people; rather it seems they are celebrating a family member at the gravesite.

WAYNE COUNTY

Blue Clay Falls

Centerville: North end of Abington Rd.

Reports of a group of people with lanterns wearing late 1800s clothing are seen walking on the road and across fields. Many investigators have reported watching them pass en mass without any member of the group acknowledging the investigators. EVP evidence includes male and female voices urging someone to continue, singing, and crying. Some investigators have speculated these are Native Americans, however, some investigators believe these are displaced people from some other source.

Crying Woman's Bridge

Dublin: Heacock Road, which is parallel to US40. The bridge is gone but where it stands is now blocked at both ends for safety reasons. The location is hard to find in summer due to overgrowth.

A woman lost her baby in an unidentified accident on the bridge. Visitors report hearing a baby cry and a woman wailing and calling for her child. Investigators have reported the names Johnny and Will.

Other variations include the woman driving a car with her baby girl next to her. Rain began to fall and the woman, unfamiliar with the roads, ran off the bridge. The woman's body was found, but not the child's. The mother's remains were reportedly buried in a Potter's field with her baby's pink blanket and pacifier.

Still other people have reported that the woman made sure the child was safe and then died, haunting the area and killing children. (Reportedly several children have drowned in the area.)

When couples used to park on the bridge, they claimed they would hear the woman's fingernails on the car and find scratches in the paint later.

Doddridge Chapel Cemetery

Centerville: Abington Township Line Road and Chapel Rd
Currently the Doddridge Chapel Cemetery Association sells copies of the cemetery records to keep the grounds and chapel.
(aka Chapel Road Cemetery and Church)

Phillip Doddridge donated the four acres for the church/cemetery and was the first person buried there. In 1816, Doddridge built a log cabin for worship in the SE corner.

Reportedly, if you park your car in the church driveway and shut off your lights and ignition, you will hear a dog whining. The temperature will drop inside the car, even during the hottest months. Other reports include adult sized handprints on car windows and vehicle, and shape-shifters outside the car that will appear on one side, disappear, then to reappear on another side.

Earlham College
Richmond: 801 National Road West

Library: Genealogy room is home to mysterious shadow figures
Grounds: Transparent figures of men and women in Quaker garb are seen walking through campus. Legend has it that on Halloween night 1857 that two students were walking across a pipe in the creek and hit their heads. They passed out and died in the shallow water. Today, if you visit the creek on Halloween night, you hear screaming and splashing in the water below.

Goshen Cemetery
Richmond: On SR 227 north of Turner Rd.

A lady in white disappears when you approach her. Footsteps follow you throughout the cemetery. Shadows and white lights dart through the area. The northeast section contains a large amounts of children. Odd thumps, bumps and temperature drops occur.

Old Burial Ground
Richmond: S. Seventh and E Streets
(aka Swicker Park)

The first non-Quaker cemetery in Richmond is home to quite a few ghost sightings. While Burials stopped in 1870, and by 1881 the cemetery was in shambles. It became a dumping ground for anything and everything. In 1881 when South E Street was extended, workers cut through the cemetery sending bodies, bones and coffins into the air. By March 1881 a ghost was seen walking around the cemetery and going to homes and tapping on windows. In April 1881 the ghost, now seen as an old man, was asked by a man named Al Bogart, "'What disturbed you?' The ghost answered, "We are on strike," replied the specter. "We have seen our graves neglected, our last resting place desecrated and made places for the living to sneer at and avoid; our tombstones are covered with moss until the inscriptions are hidden; our graves are sunken in until they are all but holes in the ground; weeds and grass grow over us and wrangle at our unfortunate condition until even the birds of the air avoid us. We are going on strike! We want shorter grass, better fences, less pasturage for cows and horses over us..."

"'We seek treatment as if we had once been human beings who helped build Richmond and make it habitable... Wandering horses and wayside cows and errant pigs disturbs us! We rest uneasy in our narrow houses, not knowing what is to come... Fences are cheap, labor is plentiful, ground is obtainable, yet we are left after our years of toil and trouble on earth, with actually not a place to lay our heads! That is why we go on strike in Richmond!'"

Once the South Side Improvement Association heard of this exchange, they offered anyone who wanted to move their family should do so. The Cemetery became a park. However, only a handful of people relocated relatives. In 1894, the workmen removed the headstones, and left the bodies. In September of that year, the newspaper reported workmen stumbling on remains. The Evening Item reports: "Upon numerous occasions the workers have come across remains; this morning marks the climax. In the huge bank that is being cut down about the center of the place, a metallic casket was dug out... The casket is five feet and four inches in length, is of solid iron and old style in shape. At the head a small iron door opens back and beneath a thin pane of glass the features of a woman are plainly to be seen. The face is in a good state of preservation. The hair, which is brownish color, is smoothed as straight across the forehead as if it had been combed but yesterday. The identity of the person is unknown... Residents on that end of town say that it has been 25 years since anybody was interred in the old cemetery, and it is possible that the body found today has been there twice that long. Hundreds of people visited the place today and were permitted to gaze... into the window of the past."

As the workman converted the site, the gravestones were recycled into south side walkways. Four years later, grass was sown. In 1899 the dedication of Swicker Park was made.

Throughout the 1900s ghosts of the graveyard have been reported and it is believed it is Richmond's early settlers unhappy with what has happened to their resting place.

Richmond Downton
Richmond: Around 6th and Main Streets

On April 6, 1968 a natural gas explosion killed 41 people and injured over 150. It was caused by a gas leak under Marting Arms Sporting Goods. A second explosion was caused by gunpowder. Twenty buildings were torn down as a result and Richmond downtown was rebuilt.

From that time, the ghosts of these people have been seen on the street and in the new buildings. Many investigators believe these are residual hauntings from people who were not ready to go.

Richmond State Hospital
Richmond: 498 NW 18th St.
(Note: This hospital is still in use by various organizations and patients receiving care are still on the grounds. If you do visit, be respectful.)

Nearly every old mental asylum has ghost stories attached to it and Richmond is no exception. Throughout the older buildings you can hear strange things. Wheels of a phantom cart are heard, as are mysterious moans and screams. Legend has it that in the old powerhouse a room in the middle, there are bloody handprints.

It's been reported that the greenhouses around the hospital are also haunted; however, this seems to be more legend. A small office with a phone is supposed to be on the grounds. If you pick up the phone and listen, an operator asks you who you want to speak with. This story also seems to be legend or the phone is no longer on the grounds or accessible.

Star Piano Building
Richmond: White River Gorge Park

This area is rumored to have been built on a cemetery, but that is nothing more than legend. The building has now been turned into an outdoor concert and event hall.

Richmond is widely known as the birthplace of jazz. As part of that birthright, the Star Piano Company, which opened in 1872, began recording records in 1915 using old equipment from a bankrupt company from Boston.

The recording company was named Gennett, thereby avoiding confusion with the piano side of the business. A groundbreaking company, Gennett recorded both black and white artists. Some of the best known jazz artists, including Louis Armstrong, recorded at the studio. History reports that the recording studio was at the south end of the company complex and when trains would roll by, all recording had to be suspended because of the noise. Eventually, Decca bought the rights to some of Gennett's recordings and in 1997, Richmond began preserving this vast jazz legacy.

Two buildings remain- the concert hall and a smaller, unkempt building. In the smaller building, there is evidence of graffiti and squatters, and the remains of some of the workers. Many people have reported male and female office workers walking in the area of the buildings in 1920s clothing. One visitor stopped to talk with a full color solid female entity and chatted about the company. The woman was quite knowledgeable. When the visitor mentioned how sad she was that there was no one specific place to get the Gennett records, the entity was puzzled, saying they were available through the company and at music stores. When the two said their goodbyes, the woman walked into one of the concert hall towers and disappeared.

Index

www.ingramcontent.com/pod-product-compliance
Lightning Source LLC
LaVergne TN
LVHW061259060426
835509LV00013B/1491